Just Magnificent

LESSONS FROM A LIFE IN GOLF

Just Magnificent
LESSONS FROM A LIFE IN GOLF

BRIAN TWITE

with *GILLIAN EDNIE*

Y B
Your Biography

www.yourbiography.com.au

First published in 2018

Y|B

Your Biography

Published in Australia by:
Your Biography
East Malvern Victoria 3145
www.yourbiography.com.au
yourbiography@optusnet.com.au
Biographer: Gillian Ednie
Editor: Steve Perkin
Cover design: Michael Bannenberg
Typesetting and design: BookPOD
Printed by: IngramSpark in Australia

A catalogue record for this
book is available from the
National Library of Australia

NATIONAL
LIBRARY
OF AUSTRALIA

Just Magnificent – Lessons from a Life in Golf
ISBN 978-0-6484300-0-1

Further copies of this book can be purchased at
www.yourbiography.com.au/BrianTwite, and

My Bookshop, 513 Malvern Road, Hawksburn Victoria 3142
www.mybookshop.com.au.

Contents

ACKNOWLEDGEMENTS

This book began as a gift to Brian Twite for his 90th birthday. It was to be just a few audio recordings of Brian's personal life story to be shared with his family as a thank-you gesture from a forever grateful golfer. Brian has had a huge impact on my golf, as he has on countless others. He has taught me to play from my teenage beginnings, throughout the many decades since, and is still successfully helping me play my best golf today. Brian has always been there with a ready remedy, a reminder, or simply his presence to swiftly restore lost alignment and renew confidence whenever needed.

However, as Brian's bigger life story unfolded, the project developed a momentum of its own. It soon became apparent that many important stories and his legacy, as a teacher and an elder in the golf club, had not been recorded and were in danger of being lost. Thanks to the contributions of so many like-minded people, his full story can now be shared with his much-loved family, friends and the wider golfing community.

Special thanks to Sadie Ann Heizer, Susie Gracey and Andrew Twite, Brian's children, his brother Terry Twite, and stepson Stephen Enright, and to the host of friends, former caddies and players for sharing their 'Brian' stories and reflections so willingly. Particular thanks also to those who helped create the book: Moira Drew, Metropolitan archivist, and club historians John Churchill and Chris Reeks of Sunningdale and King's Lynn, for sourcing historic material and photographs; John Ross and Peter Lothian for reading early drafts; Steve Perkin for editing the final manuscript; Ev Beissbarth for her overall publishing guidance; Michael Bannenberg for the cover design; and Sylvie Blair of Bookpod for the layout and typesetting. Special thanks also to Corrie Perkin who kept the project going with her vision and enthusiasm; to Peter Paccagnan and Sue Clark of Metropolitan, Graeme Ryan of the Golf Society, and Karen Harding of Golf Victoria for helping to promote the book, and to all those who have given encouragement along the way.

Finally, the biggest thank you goes to Brian Twite for telling his inside story, and for sharing his love of golf and wisdom with us all, so generously and so completely, throughout his remarkable lifetime in the game.

Gillian Ednie, biographer and player

FOREWORDS

I have known Brian Twite for over 60 years since my first visit to Australia in 1956. We met at the Ampol Tournament which was the first Australian tournament for both of us, and the first of many visits and significant wins I enjoyed in Australia over the next twenty years.

During these visits, I would visit Brian in his pro shop at Metropolitan in Melbourne to catch up even when his Club wasn't hosting a tournament that year. Brian has always been a thorough gentleman, and one of the finest club professionals you could find anywhere.

Early on in my career, I went to England to spend a week at Sunningdale Golf Club with the legendary player and teacher Arthur Lees. As Brian had also spent a long time with Arthur when he worked as his Assistant Professional at Sunningdale in the early 1950s, we had a lot in common. Every time I came to Melbourne, Arthur asked that I remember him to Brian, and I was happy to do so. Brian and I shared an enormous respect for Arthur. But more than this, we have enjoyed a special bond as friends.

Gary Player

In 1955, Metropolitan announced the appointment of Brian Twite of Sunningdale Golf Club, UK, to the position of head professional at Metro. The members were very excited at the prospect of a young enthusiastic professional coming to our club. The current pro, Mr Horace Boorer, was coming to the end of his career after nine years and wanted to go into a retail outlet. Horace was a wonderful clubmaker with an enviable reputation, but that was his main interest and he did not enjoy teaching. Brian Twite was coming to us with a wonderful record in England for both his golfing ability and his coaching methods. I was one of the young men very excited at the prospect of such a star coming to help us all with our games.

Brian arrived in late 1955. We met a few days later and immediately became friends. That friendship has lasted 63 years, and I only have praise for his gentlemanly demeanour, his friendly manner with all members, young or old, his knowledge of golf, its traditions and history, and his golfing ability and his humility.

Just mention the name Brian Twite anywhere in Australian golf circles and instantly there will be a very positive reaction of respect and admiration for this man who has added so much to the reputation of our club.

In Brian's favourite words, his long stay at Metro has been 'just magnificent'.

Robert Wade OAM

After 60 years at Metropolitan as our golf pro, a member, and more recently life member, Brian is widely acknowledged as part of the fabric of the Club. Brian is the personification of professionalism in sport. He is gifted, fair, honest and always generously acknowledges the good effort of others. When we wave to him across the fairways on Saturday mornings, or notice him having a quiet solo practice in the evenings, I know that all is well at our Club.

Brian is the Wikipedia of the Club's history. He remembers the terrain, every fairway, bunker, green, as they are now and as they were before numerous renovations.

At 92 years, Brian remains a dedicated and involved teacher. As our professional during numerous seasons, he was generous with his time, encouraging us, providing insightful individual assessments, and directions to improve our play. I remember once he demonstrated a particularly difficult shot with the blade of the club upside down and reversed. We were amused, but sure enough that shot turns up occasionally, which makes me laugh out loud. Apart from his absolute integrity and obvious talent, the secret to Brian's success is that he simply loves what he does. There is nothing more pleasing to him than to play a competitive fulfilled game with friends.

I first met Brian over 50 years ago when I had my first lesson with him. Later both he and Isabel became close friends. It has been, and continues to be, a privilege to hang out and enjoy a round of golf with a legend.

Dr Kay Leeton

There was a time, believe it or not, when club pros made and repaired clubs, played with the members, taught the game and ran their own professional shops. Most had one young apprentice to help, but Brian Twite usually had two, such was his reputation as a teacher, and no-one in the city gave as many lessons.

Club repairing is a lost art, one replaced by 'club fitting' as each year the manufacturers promise another 10 metres with a newer and better alternative to the newer and better alternative from the previous year.

Mostly golf professionals don't run their shops anymore because the clubs took them over. Even teaching is more specialised, as clubs hire pros specifically for the task.

Playing with the members? That doesn't seem to happen too much, either.

With all the burdens of the job, some of the old-school pros could be pretty grumpy old bastards. Putting up with cantankerous members was always tricky. It still is.

Teaching those without much hope of ever getting any better was never the easiest task, but Brian was the master of encouragement and picking just the right tip to send them to the tee, with at least a rudimentary level of competence and some confidence.

On every level, to be a successful, respected and much-loved pro at a club you have to be a kind person. When I first joined Metropolitan in 1975 as an 18-year-old, the next youngest player in the pennant team was Glynn O'Collins. He was 43.

My friends Clyde Boyer and John Kelly were two of the best players in the state and members at Yarra Yarra and Southern respectively. Both were busy courses and late in the day we would often meet at Metro to play.

We were all impoverished university students and Brian would happily send us out onto the usually empty course without ever thinking to charge them a green fee.

Seeing how much the club had to offer, both Clyde and John became members before long and became great contributors to the club. When people talk about 'growing the game' that is but one example of how to do it.

Few have done a better job of taking the game they love to such a wide audience all over the state than Brian Twite.

He is one of the game's most remarkable treasures. We at Metropolitan should be eternally grateful that he made the rash choice to leave Sunningdale, one of the game's greatest clubs, and come all the way to our end of the world to make our club a much better place.

Mike Clayton

I first met Mr Twite when I was introduced to him by my grandfather Bill Anketell. I was about eight or nine years old. Mr Twite was very engaging, but I found him very hard to understand with his strong English accent. My grandfather deciphered the conversation in the car on the way home and with hindsight his accent was clearly understood the second time around.

Mr Twite was a stickler for the rules and Club etiquette. I recall one day a group of us were out on the course and we were caught in torrential rain. Worried about my mother's reaction, I thought it was a good idea to tuck the cuffs of my trousers into my socks to keep them as clean as I could. Arriving back at the clubhouse Mr Twite told me in the firmest but nicest possible way that I was never to tuck my trousers into my socks again unless I was wearing plus fours.

I enjoyed lessons with Mr Twite and it became clear that he taught golf in a simple and uncomplicated manner. This simple and uncomplicated method he maintained with all golfers, from raw beginners like me to scratch golfers alike, and he continues to do so to this day.

It took me several decades to address Mr Twite as Brian which I now do, albeit sometimes reluctantly.

Brian is a remarkable gentleman who has an unlimited number of stories about golf, teaching and, perhaps more importantly, about life. Every day he communicates in an engaging and charming manner with everyone he meets.

As Club Captain I can attest that Brian has a deep connection with our wonderful Club, but we are most certainly the beneficiaries of that connection, which started on the day he arrived at the Club in 1955. The Metropolitan Golf Club has recognised Brian Twite's contribution in many ways over the years; however, it is most appropriate that the soon-to-be-constructed on-course teaching facility will be named in his honour.

Marcus Harty

Brian has been a well-respected PGA member for over 60 years spending the majority of his working life at one of Australia's premier golf clubs The Metropolitan Golf Club. Brian excelled in the area of coaching with a particular interest at the junior level via his cadet and junior scholarship programs that he conducted both locally and in regional areas. Brian has epitomised everything the Professional Golfers Association stands for during his storied career and remains a highly respected member of the Australian PGA to this day.

Much loved by The Metropolitan Golf Club members, Brian's charm, personality and personable demeanour have ensured he will always have a great place in not only the history of the PGA, and The Metropolitan Golf Club but also the Victorian Golf Industry having been inducted to the Victorian Golf Hall of Fame in 2013, an honour truly befitting of a great professional.

Gavin Kirkman, CEO, PGA

INTRODUCTION

Sunday, 3 September 1939, Leziate, Norfolk, UK

I WAS SHAKING IN MY BOOTS. I HAD MY HANDS ON THE ROPE and was ready to pull. I knew I was going to cop it, but I was ready for that, too. Everyone had heard that the Prime Minister, Neville Chamberlain, had declared war on Germany that morning. I was 13 and didn't know what it meant for the country or what it would mean for me. I only knew I couldn't go on, I had to break free.

Propelled by my own will and the strange charge in the atmosphere, I took a few deep breaths and pulled the rope as hard and fast as I could. The bells rang out wildly across the countryside, wonderfully louder than I had ever heard before – bang, clang, bang, bang. It was deafening and magnificent.

As planned, I was sacked on the spot by the vicar. Perfect. I was now free to do the only thing I wanted to do – to caddy and play golf on a Sunday, like I could on every other day of the week.

From my earliest memories, I devoted all my free time and energies to golf. I wanted to be the best I could be. I was captivated. Every part of me was driven to hit the ball further and to master every shot from wherever it lay. Little did I know then that my love of golf would become my vocation, that it would lead me to work and play on some of the best golf courses, and to meet some of the best golfers in the world, among them Gary Player, Jack Nicklaus, Arnold Palmer and Greg Norman, and lead me to a new life in Australia.

Nor could I imagine then that I would devote my adult life to teaching others to be true to themselves and to be the best that they could be, on and off the course.

Luckily for me, I found my talent early and followed it with a single-mindedness that was only interrupted by the War. Along the way I learned the greatest lessons from the greatest teachers. On the outside, as a player, it was all about how best to connect the clubhead with the ball, how to read the conditions of play – the wind, the lies on and off the fairways, the speed and borrow of the greens – and how to strategically play the game with its fixed and changing challenges.

As a teacher, it was all about seeing and listening, to find and then to build on a player's natural talents, to adapt the fundamentals to a player rather than vice versa, and to develop, and never to compromise or doubt their own inner 'hit' – their natural genius. My gift was to help them to recognise, respect and believe in their unique gifts, and express their highest potential by seeking to be the best they can, not a copy of someone else. Once that's done, my simple philosophy of golf and life has been to:

- accept the lie you are given and adapt to it as best you can;
- work around what you can't change;
- don't dwell on the past or worry about the future;
- get on with it, follow your energy, take the initiative, test new things, and the way forward will appear;
- when adversity strikes or when hit by grief, be it yours or others, just keep going, keep working and keep being you. Don't stay home and weep, continue to show up in your place for your purpose in the world. Again, accept the lie and the life you have. It may be very different to the one you wanted, but it will still be a great life because it's the one you have been given.

These simple truths have sustained me for over 90 years and teaching them to others keeps a spring in my step. I am often asked what keeps me going. For me, it's like a circle, like the game of golf itself, in which we are constantly inspired and guided by the feedback we receive to do better and to be the best we can be. We savour and build on the positives, the successes, and let the negatives go.

I love hearing about the lessons that have worked, the triumphs when a troublesome shot is mastered, a handicap is reduced, or a pennant match or grandmother's trophy is won. My reward is the recognition and the knowing that the whole system has worked: first, that my teaching is correct, second, that I have taught it correctly for that player, and finally, that the player has learnt it, practiced it and has applied it correctly on the golf course. Their lift is my lift. This is what makes me tick, this has been my purpose, and this is the story of how it has shaped my life. My hope now is that it may also shape yours.

PART ONE

GOLF IN THE KINGDOM

– CHAPTER 1 –

My earliest years

FOR ME IT ALL STARTED ON 23 AUGUST 1926, IN THE TINY English village of Leziate, Norfolk, in the United Kingdom. I was the fourth of twelve children. My father, William, and my mother, Sylvia (nee Panks), met in the local village. They both grew up in Leziate, married there in 1919 and remained living happily there all their lives.

My father worked on a vegetable farm growing peas, potatoes and beetroot, while my mother stayed home all day looking after us children.

From 1920 to 1945, there was a new Twite baby born almost every two years. In birth order, we were Theresa, Eileen, Basil, Brian, Daphne, Brenda, Shirley, Wendy, Nigel, Sadie, Keith and Terry, the last to be born in 1945. I am now the oldest as my older sisters and brother have died, as have Shirley and Keith. I have seven left. Five live in the UK, one in the US and Terry lives here in Melbourne.

Our home life was very good. There were only about eight houses in the village and about fifteen children around my age. We had a wonderful time. We all went to each other's houses to play cards and sports and got along very well with each other. In those days, there was no television, so you made your own fun and sport around the village. Fortunately, it was a very happy and a very healthy village. I'm not sure about now, but when I left, there were fifteen people over 90. They put it down to the water and turnips. There were always plenty

From left: Theresa, Eileen, Basil, and Brian seated, circa 1930

of turnips. I remember we'd just take a turnip out of the garden and eat it on the way to school.

The earliest memory I have is of playing in a sandy bunker at our neighbouring golf course. First thing in the morning, my mother would take about five of us to the nearest bunker next to the 14th green, just 100 yards down the road. She'd give us a bucket and spade and we'd spend an hour there building sandcastles, running up and down the face of the bunker and doing everything we liked.

The thing that amazed me most was that, when my mother came back to pick us up, she always brought a rake. I used to say to myself: 'What the hell has she got a rake for?' And she'd spend 10 minutes raking that bunker so it looked like we had never been in it. The members wouldn't get around to the 14th hole until two o'clock in the afternoon, so nobody from the club ever knew we played there. We used to do that once or twice a week.

Our mother was a good mother and had to be with twelve of us to look after. I remember meal times and sitting around the dinner table. Mother had a five-foot cane by her side. You would often see her reach for it and then, all of a sudden, somebody would get a hit across the knuckles. And you'd say: 'What's that for, Mum?' 'Well, if you don't know, son, you'll remember.' Years later I said to my mother: 'I often wondered why you kept hitting us.' She explained: 'Because, son, it was the only way I could keep control of you. None of you ever knew who was going to get hit next, so you all behaved.' It was all good fun. It was all good, clean-living fun.

We lived at 'Brow o' the Hill', 1 Council House, Leziate, which was a three-bedroom cottage next to the golf course. We usually slept four in a bed, two on the top and two on the bottom with our feet in the middle, which worked until we were about nine. The boys and girls were in different beds. Then two slept on the couch downstairs. Despite the lack of space, nobody slept in the sitting room which was only ever used on Sundays. In fact, we only used it for afternoon tea, which was good for me because everyone had a job to do and my job was cleaning the sitting room. I don't know why, but I was the favourite. I couldn't do anything wrong. Everybody got

Basil, Eileen and Brian, outside 'Brow o' the Hill', No 1 Council House, circa 1933

into trouble, but I never did, not from my mother at least, and I did help her wherever I could. Dad would smack us all if we were naughty, but Mum wouldn't.

We had to clean our own shoes every day, too. As part of a deal with two of my brothers and two of my sisters, I ended up cleaning five pairs of shoes a day. In return, I got to be the first to read the latest edition of *The Adventures of Rupert the Bear*, which was delivered once a week. It didn't matter what time I walked into the room, or who was reading it, the magazine was given to me. That was the deal.

Our bathroom was in an outside shed and there was no hot water. Once a week, we kids would boil the water in a kettle on the stove and take it out to the bathroom. Then we would all have a bath. It was a big deal. I didn't have a proper shower until I left home and worked on the Downham Market Airfield and I could have a proper shower every day. I loved that.

Mum made all our clothes and they all went down the line. The 14-year-old boy's clothes went down to the 12-year-old, the 12-year-old's went down to the 10-year-old. You might be five and be wearing somebody else's patched-up clothes that were five years old, too. It was all fun. Mum made her own clothes, and my sisters, when they were older, also learnt to make all their own clothes.

I was only four and a half when I started school in February 1930. It was in the middle of winter. Snow was on the ground, so it was very cold, and I only had short pants. We had to walk to school which was a mile away and Mother took us. I remember so clearly how the older school children got me into an awful lot of trouble. They taught me and the other new kids how to flick a cotton wool ball dipped in ink with a ruler at the teacher who was about six foot two and a bully. We were terrible and I got caught. The cotton wool would bleed ink on the teacher's clothes. So, on my very first day, I got a good spanking across the backside. I must have been crying when I went home because Mum asked me: 'What's wrong?' I said: 'I got hit across the bum today with a cane.' 'What for?' she asked, and when she found out, she added: 'Wait till your father comes home.' She always called him 'father'. And she said to my dad: 'Father, Brian got spanked by the schoolteacher today. I want you to go down and see the schoolmaster.' Dad said: 'Son, come into the living room', which I knew was serious. 'Now, where did he hit you?' I said: 'Across the bum.' 'Bend down, show me.' And I bent down, and he took off his belt and gave me a whack across the bum. 'Now, that'll teach you to behave yourself.' I felt even worse after that and I thought: 'Why should he hit me?' In hindsight, it was the correct thing to do and I never did it again. I behaved myself after that.

School was very good, really. It was crowded and we had 45 in each class. It was only a little village school and there were about 130

'Brow o' the Hill', 1 Council House, Leziate

17

children for three teachers. I was good at the three 'r's. My arithmetic was very good, my English was quite good, but my writing wasn't as good. Nevertheless, I still got good marks all the way through. I had to. When I got home my mother would always say: 'School report?' If it wasn't very good, you got a spank across your bottom. My main interest, however, was always elsewhere.

We were a big family to feed and we went through a lot of bread. We had a dozen loaves delivered every day, which were about half the size of today's loaves. We had toast, bread and butter or bread and jam for breakfast, sandwiches for lunch and more bread with dinner. If there was ever any left over, we gave it the pigs. We always had plenty of food because we shot all the rabbits and pheasants we needed. In addition, my parents would often kill a pig.

My mother always won a pig in the putting competition at the village Harvest Festival. She never played golf, but she'd win that damn competition year after year which was very annoying for

Ashwicken School House

the golfers in the family. As a seamstress, like Helen Kimber, she could see the line and could hit everything straight. The putting competition was held on the front lawn of the vicarage which was very flat and specially mown for the occasion. We would be looking for the borrow, but mother would just go boom, straight in the hole. She couldn't understand why we couldn't do the same.

'We all had to go to church three times on Sunday and we all had a job to do. Mum made us go until we started work, and then she said: "You decide what you want to do." Wendy was a bell ringer (and still is), Brenda and Daphne used to play the organ and I had to pump the organ. If I was in a foul mood I would hold it, so it nearly ran out of air.'

Terry Twite, brother

We spent a lot of time around the vicarage – far too much time in my opinion. On Sundays, I went to church at 11.00 in the morning, back for Sunday School at 2.30, and church again at 6.00.

All Saints Church, Ashwicken, Norfolk

19

I will never forget the last time I rang the bells. It was Sunday, 3 September 1939. The Prime Minister, Neville Chamberlain, was on the radio that morning to say that war had been declared. I was thirteen and had had enough. I remember thinking: 'That's it. How the hell can I get out of this job?' I wanted to be on the golf course to be either caddying or playing golf. I pulled the rope so hard, the bell went bang, bang, bang, and the whole village heard it. I was sacked on the spot, and off I went to play golf. I got a slap across the backside for being naughty but it was worth it.

CHAPTER 2

Finding golf

MY INTEREST IN GOLF REALLY STARTED WHEN I WAS ONLY FOUR and I found my first golf ball. I got a stick and I started knocking this ball around, and then my brothers and friends started hitting balls around, too. And I thought: 'Oh, Twitey, you're pretty good at this. You can hit this ball 10 yards further than anybody else.' I was four and I was hooked. I was hitting golf balls with practically every spare minute I had. My father didn't play golf, but he knew what a club was like and made us about four clubs from the boughs of willow trees. He shaved the branches to make little woods, shaping the clubhead from the joint or the nut where the bough joints the trunk. We played with these sticks for about four years. When we kids were too young to go on the course, we played on our own golf course.

As a village boy, if I hadn't started then, I would still have got to golf later by caddying when I was eight, but I wouldn't have had all those years of excitement of hitting a ball 30, 40 yards when I was six and seven and using an old stick.

'We were so very lucky because, across the road from where we lived, there was a large natural clearing in the forest with a big plateau. On the top of this, the village kids and Dad had made a three-hole golf course. We even had a few bunkers, but it was all sandy with lots of ups and dips. We also had see-saws made from a plank in the V of a tree a flying fox. I'll tell you what, we had a darn good life playing up there.'

Terry Twite, brother

Ball hunting and night golf

The first balls I knew were small wound balls, such as Bromfords, TeeVees, Penfolds, and Slazengers. They had a liquid centre with a thin rubber band around them, and then a thicker rubber band, and a cover. We were very good at finding them and quite often we'd find them before they stopped rolling, so we always had a good supply. We would find 20 or 30 balls a day and the members would give us a penny for each. Some would say: 'Take them back to the professional shop.' But when we took them back to the professional shop, the professional would say: 'These belong to the golf course, not to you,' and he would take them away from us. We had hundreds of balls and eventually we did send them back. We boxed them up and sent them back to Bristol and they re-covered them, so we helped recycle them.

Under the age of nine, we weren't allowed on the course in the daytime, so we would often go out and play in the moonlight. The police would come and take the clubs off us, and we'd have to go to the station and pick them up the next morning, and then we'd go straight back on the golf course again. This happened once every four or five weeks. The police eventually got fed up and stopped coming. We weren't doing any harm, and we looked after the course.

In those days, King's Lynn was a very elite golf club. Only millionaires and very wealthy people were members. The captain at the time was Wilfred Thomas, who owned Middleton Hall, which was only seven miles away. He didn't come by car, he came by Tiger Moth, and landed it on the fairway. That's how wealthy the club was then. After the War, of course, things changed and the local people became members. But before the War, it was a very elite club. It was like Metropolitan Golf Club was 50 years ago.

Becoming a caddy

I was only eight when I was asked to caddy. We had 40 caddies at King's Lynn Golf Club. Every player had a caddy then, and they were running short of men, so they asked all the youngsters to caddy, and we did. My older brother, Basil, and later all my brothers, and about seven friends from the village, all caddied and played golf together.

We got threepence a round while the men got two shillings. I used to caddy for an old fellow named Billy Sadler who played off a handicap of 20. He was the richest man in the club and the meanest, too, I soon discovered. Before long, I said to the professional: 'I don't want to caddy for this fellow.' He asked why not and I said: 'Well, every time he loses a ball he takes a penny off me. So, if he loses two balls, I only get a penny. When he loses three balls, I get nothing.' He looked at me and said: 'Well, son, let me tell you this. He plays with TeeVee golf balls which are four for a shilling. Now you must have dozens of TeeVee balls at home. If I was in your shoes, I would put three in my pocket, and every time he loses a ball, you drop one in the rough and say: "Here it is, sir," which I did. We never lost a golf ball again. After three months, he said: 'Twite, you are the best ball finder I've ever come across. I'm going to increase your wage to the men's wage', which was two shillings a round. I caddied for him every Saturday and Sunday for three years and we never lost a ball. I was the

Golf balls of the day, circa 1940s

richest kid in the village, but I didn't spend it. I gave a shilling to my mother, which helped pay for all the loaves of bread we needed each day, and I kept a shilling.

I played with my home-made clubs until I was about nine or ten. Then my dad somehow got some old clubs, and I was given a 'spoon' (a 3 wood) as my driver, a 'jigger' (like a 4 iron), a 'mashie' or 'niblick' (a 7 iron), and a putter. For me, the jigger was the finest club ever made. The head was 4 inches long, 1 inch in depth, with the loft of a 4 iron and the length of a 2 iron. It was magnificent. You could do anything you liked with it. I had a driver, a jigger, a mashie niblick and a putter. I used these four clubs until I was fourteen and my first handicap was nine.

Basil and I played every day except Sunday. We also played with Henry Hudson, who lived next door and John Springfield, who was two houses away. There were four of us who'd play at every opportunity we had. We'd all meet by the 14th green and go from there. We'd play 15, 16 and 17, then 5 to 8 and finally 10 back to 14. We would skip the holes where we could be seen from the clubhouse.

The King's Lynn Club House in 1927

Learning to play

Mostly we learnt from each other, by copying other people's swings and teaching ourselves by trial and error. While we were waiting for jobs in the caddies' yard, we would mimic our player's swings. 'Henry swings like this, Tom swings like this, George swings like this,' and then we would copy whichever ones we thought hit the ball the best. Then we would practice various shots around the willow tree between the caddies' yard and the golf course. We would hit low shots under and through the tree, and high shots over the tree, and try to retrieve them 50 yards away. It was great fun. And that's how we learned to control the ball and play half shots, and full clubs and all sorts of things.

Jack Lovelock's lessons

The only formal golf teaching we had as young caddies was from the club professional, Jack Lovelock. Every now and again, when I was about twelve or thirteen, Jack would take three of us aside and talk to us about how we should conduct ourselves, how the swing works and what we should do on the golf course.

Jack focused on four swing fundamentals. The first thing he taught us was to grip the club correctly. 'If you haven't got a good grip, you can't play golf.' It was that simple. 'Both Vs (the lines between the thumb and first finger made by both hands on the grip) must always be pointing up to the right shoulder.'

The second important thing he said was that thumbs point up to the sky on the backswing.

Third was the timeless favourite: 'Keep your head still.'

The fourth was to make sure that when you hit the ball, you're looking over the right shoulder. Don't allow the head to ever get ahead of the shoulder. Another way to think of this is on the backswing, you should have your head, left shoulder and left knee in line and when you hit the ball, you should have your right head, right shoulder and right knee in line.

In addition to the grip, thumbs up, head still, and hit with your head over your right shoulder, the only other thing Jack said was: 'Be confident in what you're doing. Don't hesitate.' If you hesitate, you are lost. If you're confident in your swing, even if you don't hit it quite right, it doesn't matter because you're still working on your core fundamentals. But if you start fiddling around with it, and are not confident, everything falls apart.

Jack also had some advice on putting. He always said: 'Stand up and keep your eyes still.' He meant not just to keep your head still, but keep your eyes still and focused on just one point, a dimple on the ball for example.

Unfortunately, I didn't have a priority on putting when I was young. My brother Nigel did, and he was a very good putter, mainly, I thought, because he missed more greens than I did. I'd hit 16 greens out of 18 and so often I could three-putt and still have a par. My focus and effort were on driving, which was probably wrong. I really should have spent more hours putting. I hit thousands of balls with the driver and that's why I've always been a very good driver. For example, on the fifth hole at King's Lynn, a par-five, we had bunkers at 185 yards, which every course had in those days. I'd take 50 balls to that fifth tee and I would try my hardest to get over that damn bunker. And they'd drop short into the bunker. Then suddenly one went over and from that day on I never missed. Every shot was over the bunker.

At fourteen, I'd hit it 185 yards over the bunker and it would run another 30 yards, so my length was 240 yards. But as I grew stronger from working in 'the Sandpit' – the local sand mine – I was hitting my driver on average 275 yards. I'd hit it say 230 and it would run 40. I was the longest hitter in the golf club.

We had the small balls and the persimmon woods with beautiful hickory shafts. I hardly ever missed a drive and my iron shots were magnificent, too, especially my long irons. Later in life, I could hit all my 2 irons within 10 feet of the hole.

Leaving school and starting work

In those days, when you got to the age of fourteen, you could either leave school or go to the King's Lynn High School. In 1940, I decided to leave school, start earning some money and keep playing golf. The war had been going for 13 months by then. I decided to go to work with my father. He worked in the Sandpit, at Leziate, which was the biggest sand quarry in Europe. It employed 300 people and was 150 feet deep. It was hard work but I didn't mind it. It was my job.

Ten trucks were brought in to move 10 tonnes of sand, a tonne of sand in every truck, four times a day. We had to shovel the sand into heaps and then push it down a little hopper where it would be washed, cleaned, dried and sent away every day of the week to make munitions and other important things for the wareffort. I was only there for 12 months, but shovelling 40 tonnes of sand a day really built up my muscles and strength.

CHAPTER 3

Becoming a scratch golfer

IN 1940, I WON THE CADDIES' CHAMPIONSHIP, CALLED THE Fermoy Cup, at King's Lynn, which changed everything for me. I had a first-round par of 75 in the morning and a 72 (three under) second round in the afternoon. I was on a nine handicap, so they dropped me to scratch immediately, because you can't be three under the card and stay on a nine handicap.

Billy Sadler, one of the first players I caddied for and was by then aaaged 81, made the presentation. He said: 'Twite, here is the cup for the caddies' championship and I am also going to give you my new set of clubs.' He was struggling with his health and couldn't play anymore, so he gave me his set of Slazenger Gradidge golf clubs, which were the best in the country. They included a driver, a spoon, which is the 3 wood, and a baffy, which is equal to a rescue club today, followed by a 2, 3, 4, 5, 6, 7, 8, and 9 iron, wedge, sand iron, a putter and a beautiful leather bag. I was so excited. It was one of my all-time favourite days. Even to have one new club was tremendous, but to have a whole new set was unbelievable. I felt like the luckiest kid in the country. I was the only kid in the village with a full set of clubs, and a new set, too. Everybody was jealous and wanted to borrow them, but I didn't let them. I wasn't going risk losing them. My parents were less excited. Dad just said: 'Well done, son,' and that was all.

From then on my golf skyrocketed. I didn't have more than a 73 for two years. It was easy to be on scratch because the course was so easy. We had six par fives which ranged from 460 to 520 yards. If you hit the ball 250 yards every time, and you hit straight, you were on most greens in two, or if you were not on the green, you'd be alongside it, so you only need a chip and a putt. We had four par fours which ranged from 330 to 360 yards. We could reach most of these from the tee because the ground was so dry, or you were left with just a little sand iron on to the green. The course was later extended by 500 yards, but again, in the summer when the ground was so dry, the ball just flew a mile. So to get it around in 72 was simple.

We caddies had our own handicapping system which was based on the most recent score you had in the monthly caddies' tournament and a junior event. It meant that I played off scratch most of the time. If I did have a bad score and my handicap went out, I soon got it back with a par or sub-par score the next time I played.

As a caddy, we could become artisan members which was a second-grade member with limited playing rights. We could only play before 9.00 am and after 5.00 pm, but we could play in the junior tournaments. At King's Lynn, I remember often winning the caddies' competition we held between ourselves every month. We just got a couple of balls as prizes if we won.

We had 10 junior caddies and 30 adult caddies, half of whom were full-time. I could have become a full-time caddie at King's Lynn, but I never would have. It would be too frustrating because I knew very well that I could play better than all of them but would not be allowed to give them any technical advice. I would also have to travel all over the country to other courses and I was too young to do that.

Moving to Downham Market Airfield

My golf was great, but my earnings were not. I was only earning 10/6 a week at the Sandpit. After I had been there for a year, I thought I should get a raise. I asked, but they wouldn't give me one. At the time an RAF airfield in Downham Market, 25 miles away, was being built for Stirling bombers and Wellington bombers. I saw they were advertising for people, so I went over and got a job there at £3 5s a week. I went from 10/6 to £3 5s a week, but I had to cycle 25 miles there and 25 miles back. It took over an hour, so I couldn't play golf nearly as often. Then I took up the chance to stay at the airfield. We were told: 'There are 500 people on this airfield in little units of 10 by 12 with a bed and a washbasin. If you like, you can stay here.'

We became very friendly with all the people, including the test pilots, who used to come over and chat to us. They said they would love to take us up for a flight but couldn't because the airfield wasn't in operation, which didn't happen until 1943. However, they did show us the maps and photos of what the land looked like from 5000 feet. It was such a different view of the world. I could see all the way to Cambridge. It was fantastic.

CHAPTER 4

Joining the Navy

By 1942, THE WAR WAS IN FULL SWING AND BASIL AND MY OLDER sisters had signed up, so I thought I should, too. I was still only sixteen, so I put my age up by two years and joined the Royal Navy. My eldest sister, Theresa, was in the Air Force, Basil was in the Army and my next sister, Eileen, was in the Women's Auxiliary Territorial Service

Brian in navy uniform when at sea

Brian in army uniform when on shore

(ATS), the women's branch of the British Army. So I thought, 'Well Twitie, you better join the Royal Navy and make it one of each.'

I went to Cambridge to sit the Navy exam. When I was asked for my birth certificate, I simply replied: 'I haven't got it. I couldn't find it.' I passed my exam and was told: 'Right, you can go to Chatham Naval Base for training in three weeks.' I was very excited and pleased with the news and went home for the weekend and told Mum. 'Mum, I'm joining the Navy on Monday.' She said: 'Oh no you're not. You wait till Dad comes home.'

Then when my father came home, Mum said: 'Father, Brian's joining the Navy on Monday. I want you to stop him.' Dad had had a few beers, as he always did before he came home, and he looked at me, and looked at my mother, and then looked at me again, and said nothing.

Mum said: 'Well, Dad?'

'Well,' Dad said, 'if the little bugger wants to go, let him go.' So off I went and joined the Navy. I would have joined up even if my father had said no, as I already had all my papers and my train ticket and was packed and ready to go.

I knew nothing about the Navy. I had never been on the water or even been swimming before, but I didn't see that as a problem. We did our training and, of course, you had to pass a swimming test. There were two of us who still couldn't swim, so we got one of the good swimmers to talk to the instructor about helping us and while he was outside, we managed to walk in and stamp 'Passed swimming test' on our cards.

I really learnt to swim when I was posted to the Mediterranean not much later. While we were out on a patrol, we'd stop the boat and hop overboard and have a swim. I found it much easier to swim in salt water than in fresh water, and it was a lot warmer, too. It was an exciting time for me as a teenager.

My three months of training started off with six weeks at HMS *St Christopher* (a Royal Navy Coastal Forces training base), near Fort William in Scotland. We trained on motor speedboats, motor launches and MTBs (motor torpedo boats), and we learnt to fire torpedoes.

Then we were sent to Newhaven, in southern England, where I was put on a motor patrol boat. Next,

Brian in uniform, 1943

we went to Milford Haven, in Wales, where we joined a ship which was the first of three to go across the Bay of Biscay to Gibraltar. The weather was so rough that instead of the normal three-day passage, the journey took seven days. I didn't have second thoughts about joining the Navy during that very difficult crossing, but I did have second thoughts about eating. I couldn't eat for a week. The only food was hard biscuits, and every time I ate, everything came back up. I can still remember the terrible feeling of being on that heaving ship.

I spent the next three and a half years in the Mediterranean until the war finished in 1945. My role was a gunner on a motor patrol boat. There were only twelve men on board, so everyone changed roles every three months. I was on the gun for three months, then chef for three months, then on depth charges for three months. Being on the gun was my favourite job, and I got to shoot it quite a lot, but I wasn't sure if I ever hit anything. We'd creep along the shoreline under cover of darkness, close enough to see lights on the shore, then bang away with the gun and quickly leave the scene. That happened in Sicily.

From Gibraltar, where my squadron first arrived in the Mediterranean, we went to our naval base in Bizerte, in Tunisia, because the Americans had come into North Africa for the fight against the Axis powers (Germany and Italy). Then we went to Malta and left there to become involved in the invasion of Italy through Sicily. Next, we went to the Dardanelles and were the first squadron into Dubrovnik, in what was then Yugoslavia. We finished up in Trieste, in north-eastern Italy, and then returned to Malta. After that, we went through the Anzio beachhead and were the first allied naval ships to sail into Venice.

Subsequently, we were based at a little island called Ischia, about five miles from Capri. Mostly we did patrol work, but sometimes we also landed intelligence-gathering parties on the beach on different parts of the islands, such as Corfu, and then collected the same party three or four days later. I enjoyed that work. We were in contact with people in the other ships, but most of the time we were on patrol, either hunting for submarines, picking up people and landing them on different shores and then picking them up again. It was quite dangerous work, but exciting. We were always on alert and looking for U-boats in the Mediterranean. We would drop depth charges if we thought we had one and up would come all the dead fish for breakfast.

The Yugoslavs used the British Navy to transport men and materials, but especially to make landings on the islands of Dalmatia to liberate them from German occupation. I saw quite a lot of action then, a lot of shelling. There were Germans on one side and us on the other. The local partisans knew every foot of the islands and knew where the Germans were. They were magnificent, and when the

Germans looked like they'd find us, the partisans would simply say: 'Don't worry, you just follow us.' To me, it was like hunting. My father used to take us rabbit hunting on the farm, although we children were not allowed to use a gun. Dad did all the shooting.

We were not involved in direct combat very much, but we did have a few close shaves. For example, because we were a patrol boat, we only had Bren and Oerlikon guns, so we were not allowed to attack the German boats which had much bigger two- and three-inch guns.

Nevertheless, we did attack a German boat one night. We ran it ashore and sank it and were reprimanded for doing that, but we also got commended.

Motor Patrol Boat 468, Bari, December 1944

People have asked me if I was afraid during my war service. Yes, I was afraid at times. Mostly I never thought about it because I felt safe with my team, but when I did, I never let it show. I was on the same ship for three years and we became a very good, tight team. Once appointed to one of those small ships, you stayed there. The service limit in the Mediterranean was two and a half years, and then you'd be transferred back to England. But because the war was nearly finished, we stayed longer. I was decorated with several medals for my service, including the Italian Medal, the African Star and the silver medal everyone got for war service.

Like many people, I didn't get demobbed until well after the war finished. On returning to England, I was sent to the naval base at Chatham and then sent to Newcastle upon Tyne, where they were building the aircraft carrier HMS *Triumph*. We were there for six months, refuelling the ship and getting it ready to sail. Then the crew came to the ship, and, to my great surprise, my brother Keith was part of that crew. They went on the Murmansk convoys to Russia.

I finally returned home in April 1946, at the age of twenty. Keith was demobbed two years later. All my siblings came back and had to find work after the war. Basil, who was shot in Burma, got a job driving a little locomotive at the Sandpit. My sister Eileen became a governess at Dr Barnardo's Home, in London, looking after 30 children. Theresa got married and worked on a farm. Daphne also got married. The rest of my brothers and sisters worked on farms around Leziate where we grew up.

The aircraft carrier HMS Triumph

– CHAPTER 5 –

Becoming a golf club professional

I DIDN'T MISS GOLF OR EVEN THINK OF IT WHILE I WAS AWAY IN the navy. I always had other things on my mind. I never thought about golf being my career, either, or about any career. Quite frankly, I never thought about what my life would bring. Each day was a different day. You could be shot and your life was liable to end at any moment. Golf to me then was just a sport, a pastime, and there was no time for sport in the navy.

Once I was home, I took up golf again, and in a short time I got back to scratch. From 1946 to 1948, I worked on the farm and played golf or caddied whenever I could. I became secretary of the King's Lynn Caddies' Club – a post previously held by my brother Basil – and played in all the caddies' and artisans' tournaments as I had done before the war.

I remember winning the prestigious Bardell Trophy for King's Lynn caddies one year, which was reported in the paper. I was three-under with five birdies and an eagle in the morning and one-under in the afternoon.

We had a monthly caddies' competition for a few golf balls which I often won too.

I was the best of the 40 caddies at King's Lynn and was usually in the top four or five when we played against all the caddies in the area – there might be 80 in the field. I think I won two or three tournaments. The prize for winning was a silver cup or a tray, which I

Young caddie's easy win in Bardell cup

BRILLIANT golf by 22-year-old Brian C. Twite, wearing his familiar green beret, won him the Bardell cup in the annual competition of Lynn Caddies' Club on Sunday.

Eleven members of the club competed over 36-holes, but Twite had a runaway win. He was playing off what proved to be the ridiculous handicap of 9, which gave him a score of 128 net for the two rounds.

His gross scores of 72, three strokes under the Leziate par of 75, and 74 were proof of his outstanding qualities as a young golfer.

Twite, a "natural" golfer, practices hard and has made remarkable progress. His round of 72 included five "birdies" (at the 2nd, 9th, 15th, 16th and 17th holes) and an "eagle" 3 at the long eighth hole.

would give to Mum. You weren't allowed to take money.

We played in all the local tournaments we could, and I would always try to win. We didn't have to pay to enter, we just sent off a form but then we had to cycle the 20 or 30 miles with our clubs on our backs to get there, play 36 holes and cycle home. We played at Hunstanton, Brancaster, Gog Magog Golf Clubs, in Cambridge, and the Royal Norwich Golf Club. We'd do that every weekend.

I remember one particular trip with my uncle. We rode all night and got there just in time to tee off. I started with a birdie three, then an eleven, followed by a birdie four, a nine on the next, with run of fours to finish the nine. I came home in 31 for a 78 and had a 71 in the afternoon. I was so tired in the morning, I hit three out-of-bounds on the second and another two on the fifth, but then settled down. I was so tired in the evening I feel asleep three times in the dark on the way home. It didn't stop me. I played in tournaments every weekend, and I won quite a few of them. There were a lot of good golfers among these young men in their early 20s, so I wasn't always the winner.

My parents were pleased and always expected me to do well. I remember Mum would say: 'You've got to win, son, you're the best.' But they never thought golf was any more than a pastime. I don't think they had any thought of me turning professional until I did.

Abbeydale Golf Club

Contemporary photograph of Abbeydale Golf Club

One day, soon after the Bardell Cup win, the professional at King's Lynn Golf Club, Jack Lovelock, and the club's manager, came up to me and said: 'Twite, we've been watching your golf. You're too good to be working on the farm. Why don't you take up professional golf?' I said I'd like to, but I didn't know how to go about it. The manager said: 'Well, wait a minute' and he got on the phone. Then he said: 'My

Chased off Lynn course as boy— now golf 'pro'

Brian Twite, 22-year-old three-handicap member of the Caddies' Club at King's Lynn Golf Club, has long cherished an ambition to become a golf professional. His wish comes true this week.

Tomorrow he takes up the appointment of assistant professional to J. H. Atkinson, professional to the Abbeydale Golf Club, Dore, near Sheffield.

Except for a spell in the Navy during the war, Brian has lived all his life near the King's Lynn golf course at Leziate.

Ever since he was old enough to swing a club he has been knocking a golf ball about. Often as a youngster, too young to become a caddy, he was chased off the course. He returned at the first opportunity—a club in his hand and a ball in his pocket.

Brian Twite

Since he came out of the Navy he has been working on the land and devoting his spare time to playing golf.

He became secretary of the Caddies' Club at Leziate, and last year won the caddies' 36-hole competition for the Bardell Cup with gross scores of 72 and 74—a total of four shots below bogey. His best practice round in 68.

"This is a wonderful opportunity for Brian to make good in his ambition," says Jack Lovelock, professional to the Lynn club.

Arthur Lee, British Ryder Cup golfer, was at one time assistant at Abbeydale.

friend in Sheffield, Harold Atkinson, head professional at Abbeydale Golf Club, needs a professional, a training professional. I've arranged for you to have a meeting on Monday.'

So I went to Sheffield. The course was 20 miles away and I took a bus to Sheffield and then to the golf course. There were quite a few other boys there with me. We were paired. I was with the club captain and Harold Atkinson, the professional. I had 32 for the first nine which included three birdies and an eagle. The next best was 35. And I thought: 'I've got a good chance to get this position,' and sure enough, following afternoon tea, I was selected. I started in April 1947.

Three weeks after, when I was playing with the captain again at Abbeydale, I found out why. He said: 'Twite, do you know why I selected you for this position? It was because you were the only person in the group who had clean shoes, and I'm an army captain. Clean shoes tell me something about the person. That's the only reason you got in.'

Living in Sheffield

I was lucky to be offered lodgings with one of the Abbeyfield members, Mr Ernest Horten, who was on the committee. I stayed with him for four years. I soon discovered he owned a huge cutlery factory in Sheffield and employed 300 people. He lived with his wife, and two sons and a daughter who were all younger than me, in a big double-storey house. We all had a really good time together and I was very well looked after.

I learnt all aspects of being an assistant golf professional at Abbeydale from Harold Atkinson, who was an excellent club-maker. First of all, he taught me to make woods. In those days, it was quite a skill, and all done by hand. You had to buy a block of wood and then you'd say: 'Well, this fellow wants 10 degrees loft on this club.' So you'd find a similar wood to that already made and say: 'I'm going to make it like that.' You'd then copy the shape by sculpting the block of wood with a hammer and chisel. The first time I made a wood I spoiled the head. I put it in the lathe and just as I started to use the chisel, the whole thing tore apart. I quickly learnt that you've got to look at it and see where the grain is first, and then you file it with the grain. I shaved it against the grain, so it cost me 5 shillings.

In those days, we had hickory shafts. The company salesmen would come in with 100 hickory shafts and Harry might pick only 10 of them. Every shaft had to feel the same and be the same width. It was a big deal. It took 12 months to even know what sort of shaft you wanted. When you were picking out the shafts, you had to spring them back and see how far they could bend. You had to test every shaft of the 100 before picking out only 10 or 12. It was an art. Then you had to match them to the person.

The irons were much easier. We could buy the iron heads already made and just put a hickory shaft into them. Later we could also buy the wooden heads as they were mass produced. Instead of taking three or four weeks to make a wood, it only took three or four days because you just had to put the shaft in and then stain and polish the head.

While I didn't learn too much about how to teach from Harold Atkinson — we all developed our own teaching style — he did help me with a few fundamentals for my own swing. He saw that my right hand was too far under the shaft. It took me three months to get it on top.

George Duncan also gave me some key advice I have never forgotten. I was playing at Royal Liverpool Golf Club, at Hoylake, in the Northern Championship. I had made myself a really big driver, just as big as they are today, which I hit off the fairway, too. We used to make all our own 'woodies' as we called them then. I was topping this big driver, when a guy in a mackintosh and cap came up to me and he said: 'What's up, son?' I said: 'I can't hit the damn thing off the ground.' 'Give it to me,' he said, and he put a ball on the ground and he hit it 200 yards down the fairway. 'Nothing wrong with the club, son, but let me tell you one thing. Swing through the ball, not at the ball.' So I swung through it and hit a couple of good shots. I finished 71, 70, to finish second. And guess who presented the tournament prizes? The old fellow with a mackintosh and cap, George Duncan, the 1920 British Open champion.

I still hear him saying: 'Remember son, always swing through the ball and don't swing at it.' I learnt to hit my driver off the deck this way and it has become my signature shot. I taught my students to swing through the ball in the same way. The ball is just there. You just happen to swing through it. But when you try to hit it, that's when things go wrong.

I did have a vision that I would like to be a great golfer. In between teaching and club making, I played in all the tournaments and pennant competitions I could. But when you play tournament golf, like I did at Royal Portrush in Northern Ireland, you had to think again. It was blowing a gale and there were 156 to qualify. I shot 71-72 at Hoylake to get there, but I had two 81s at Portrush and missed the cut by six shots. It was only through putting, but I thought: 'No more, this is terrible.' I went back to Abbeydale to become a good teacher because I knew everybody wanted lessons. 'My life now,' I decided, 'is not going to be in playing tournament golf. It's going to be in teaching and becoming a club professional!'

Brian on the first hole at Abbeydale, 1951

Brian playing pennant for Abbeydale against the home team at Dorrtotley Golf Club, Sheffield, 1951

The opportunity to be a playing professional wasn't really there in those days. There was a professional circuit, but I didn't have the money or the sponsors. It cost £25 to enter a tournament and then you had to travel and stay in a hotel. I just couldn't afford it. When you're earning £3 5s a week and having to pay £2 5s for board and lodgings, you just couldn't do it. I didn't have the time, either, because I was teaching seven days a week.

Sunningdale Golf Club

I was at Abbeydale for four years before I was offered another position, again one that I did not have to apply for. Arthur Lees, a world-class champion golfer and renowned Ryder Cup player, asked me to go down to Sunningdale to be his head teaching professional.

Contemporary photograph of the iconic clubhouse at Sunningdale

Sunningdale Golf Club, in Berkshire, and about 30 miles (48 km) south-west of London, was, and still, is the best course in England.

I had known Arthur for five years and he had also been an assistant professional in Sheffield, at Lees Hall Golf Club which was only 3 miles (5 km) from Abbeydale. He was famous not only for being one of the finest golfers in the country, but also for being one of the more modest and unassuming players. To me he was also the greatest of teachers and an ideal role model. Arthur was the first person who really taught me how to look at people and their swings. He would say: 'Pick why that fellow's doing this,' or 'Why is this girl doing that?' 'Don't try,' he'd say, 'to manufacture anything. Don't change the natural ability of the swing. If somebody swings the club naturally, build around it.'

Portrait of Arthur Lees hanging in the clubhouse from A History of Sunningdale Golf Club 1900 – 2000 by John Whitfield, 2000

Now Twite Goes To Sunningdale

ANOTHER young professional golfer is leaving Sheffield. Brian Twite, 26-year-old assistant at Abbeydale, joins Arthur Lees as an assistant at Sunningdale at the beginning of April.

Twite, who is a native of King's Lynn, joined Abbeydale four years ago and has made good progress as a player, teacher, and clubmaker.

In 1951 he was runner-up in the north-west assistants' tournament at Fairhaven, quarter-finalist in the Gor-Ray tournament, and runner-up in the Sheffield open; last year he was third in the Yorkshire foursomes. His speciality is iron play.

As a boy of five he was handling golf clubs at King's Lynn, but during the war years lost touch with the game. When 16 he joined the Navy and served as a gunner in an M.T.B. for three years in the Mediterranean, taking part in the invasions of Sicily and Italy.

And that's what I've always done, and it's always been successful.

Arthur stressed that everybody is different, but the fundamentals are the same the world over. It doesn't matter where you are, you have to incorporate the fundamentals into the ability of the person. You don't teach one method for everyone. You adapt the fundamentals to the tall, the overweight, the small, the big, the strong and the weak. They can't all swing a club the same way. The swing is built around the individual, but today everybody is trying to get the same swing, which means it's manufactured. You cannot force the player to adapt to the fundamentals. The fundamentals must be adapted to the player.

To help players find their natural swing, Arthur would get them to practice throwing a ball first. I remember watching him give a lesson to the whole Ryder Cup team. He had them throwing balls 30, 40 metres for a half an hour before they hit a ball, because when you throw a ball you're not thinking...turn the shoulder, turn the hip, do this and do that. Then you put a golf club in your hand and you do the same thing. Swinging a club is very simple if you just allow yourself to swing the club. But if you try and manufacture something, the swing will always fall apart because it's not natural.

Arthur was also very strong on 'keeping those eyes still', which meant more than just keeping your head still. He would pick a particular spot on the ball to hit when putting. It could be five, six, or seven o'clock at the back of the ball (six o'clock being the centre back of the ball) depending on the borrow. If the green ran away to the left, you should hit the ball at seven o'clock to counter the slope, and if it sloped to the right, you hit the ball at five o'clock.

Arthur was one of the most respected players and club professionals in England. And because he was a world-class golfer, he had full rights on the golf course and in the golf club which was very rare for a club professional in those days, and was made an honorary member in 1956. The only other club professional I knew who could play on the course was John Jacobs from Lindrick. He was so highly regarded that he was made a life member of the Lindrick Golf Club when he retired, which was remarkable.

Teaching at Sunningdale

We had everything at Sunningdale. It was a big operation and we had a very good pro shop. Upstairs, Adam White had 15 people working for him making golf clubs. Then there was the caddy master, James Sheridan, who had his own office and looked after 60 caddies. Arthur Lees had his own office and there were large rooms for club storage and buggies.

As an assistant professional, I mainly taught lessons and helped run the shop. Club-making was secondary for me. As the head teaching professional, I was also responsible for the other three assistant professionals, Jimmy Martin, John Pritchard and David Bellamy, who report to me. We all had nicknames. Jimmy was called The Reverend because he was Irish, a smoother talker and a great swearer. John was known as The Prick because he was an arrogant public-school boy. He was the greatest golfer and knew it and didn't mind his nickname which he wore as a badge of honour. David was called Girly because he was a ladies' man, he got on so well with the girls in the kitchen, I was known as The Cardinal because I could speak to everyone and got on with them all.

We got on very well together, too, and had a weekly conference to share progress. This included feedback from members on how their lessons were going. We worked long hours and for as long as there was daylight. In summer, we worked from 6.45 am to 9.45 pm, seven days a week for a wage of 5 shillings, plus 50 per cent of the profit we made on lessons. The winter hours were 9.00 am to 5.30 pm.

I loved teaching, especially when I could really help people overcome obstacles with their golf. Sometimes, my task was just to get them to play at all. There was one Sunningdale family – the Chitchleys – who were exceptional golfers except for the youngest, a 12-year-old boy called Ian. The father, General Chitchley, was on scratch, his wife was on scratch and their daughter was on a one handicap. They brought the young boy along for lessons and said: 'Brian, he's not interested in golf. Try and get him interested in golf.' He wasn't interested because all he heard at home was how good they all were, and he didn't think he could ever be as good. Not long after, the chauffeur-driven Rolls Royce arrived and dropped off the lad. He hit a couple of balls and topped them a foot or two. I picked up the balls with a club-head. 'I want to do that,' he says. So for one hour, I taught him how to pick up balls with a club-head. The mum arrived and he proudly showed off what he could do. Two years later, he was on scratch and much later he was playing in the World Cup team and later became a commentator for the BBC. He just needed the confidence to know that, if he could do something they couldn't do, he would be good enough to play golf as well.

The film stars

As Sunningdale was one of the best clubs in Britain, you had every film star in the country wanting to be a member. I used to give lessons to Glynis Johns, one of the sexiest girls you'd ever come across. She was the mum in *Mary Poppins* and she had a sultry voice. She was gorgeous. Then there was Sylvia Syms. She was also a gorgeous 21-year-old actress when I taught her.

Glynis Johns   *Sylvia Syms*

John Hale and Michael Medwin were also regulars. Before I left Sunningdale, they were in a show in London called *The Truth and Nothing but the Truth*. They said: 'Brian, we're going to take you up to London to see the show. You stay in our unit and we'll take you to the train next morning.' So I went up to see the show and dinner, then went back to the unit. There were about 20 of us, drinking and carrying on until five in the morning. They woke me up at six and put me on the train. That was a big highlight for me.

I also played quite a bit of golf with the inspirational Douglas Bader, the World War II flying ace who lost both his legs, and the great actor Kenneth Moore, who looked exactly the same as he looked on the screen.

Douglas Bader

Kenneth Moore

The caddies

I didn't have much to do with the caddies at Sunningdale because we had a caddy master, Jim Sheridan. I did learn one thing from Jimmy, though, when I had to look after the caddies for a fortnight when he went on holiday. Every week, I had to suspend four caddies for a week. He would give me the numbers and I would tell the caddies: 'This week, it's number 10, 20, 30 and 25,' and they'd just walk off. I asked him: 'Why do you suspend them, Jimmy?' and, being a Scotsman, he replied: 'It's the only bloody way I can control them. They know that somebody is going to be suspended for a week.' They didn't take it personally; there were 60 caddies and it was just taken as part of a roster. It reminded me of the way my mother kept control of us with her long and unpredictable cane. They were so well trained; the caddies were never suspended for any other reason.

Jimmy controlled the whole thing. If he didn't want you to have a caddy, you wouldn't get a caddy. Yet everybody who knew Jim loved him. He was there for over 50 years and was the first caddy master to have his portrait painted, and it's a large portrait which still hangs in the bar. Jim has also written a book on his time at Sunningdale called *Sheridan of Sunningdale, My Fifty-Six Years as Caddie-Master*, published in 1967.

The professional tournaments

The professional staff were expected to work full-time at the club and play in the professional tournaments. One of the most important tournaments I played in during my time at Sunningdale was the Open Assistants' Golf Tournament at Coombe Hill in Surrey. The tournaments were very well reported in those days, with all the qualifying results, matchplay scores and the highlights written up in the paper. I even made the headlines a couple of times.

The second year I played in 1954, I shared the first-round lead with Tony Harmon with a 69 and a 'remarkable' 33, three under, on the back nine. Three under doesn't sound like a lot, but Coombe Hill was a very tight golf course in those days. Anything off line or too long was punished as the fairways were thickly lined with rhododendron trees, and there were masses of two-foot-high bluebells behind most greens. I went on to qualify and win my first round in the morning. I was two down in the afternoon and turned this around and to win after holing a 20-foot chip down a bank on the 12th. I was then in the semi-finals which I lost to Peter Mills 2 and 1. He then lost to Jimmy Martin, who worked under me at Sunningdale, in the final. Jimmy was an Irishman and a fabulous golfer. He won the Irish Open and several other tournaments.

The next year I represented Sunningdale at the DAKS Sunningdale Open Tournament with my fellow assistant professional John Pritchard, where we chalked up a local-boys-make-good story by leading the second round. John came in with a 70 in the second round and I came in with a 68. I had never hit the ball or handled the weather so well. The newspaper said:

> Norfolk lad Twite mocked all the prophets who said the day was too tough for anyone to crack 70 on the wind-swept new course. He handed in a 68 to jump within a shot of the maestro Henry Cotton and join Bobby Locke on the 143 mark.

I finished less well with a 75 and 73, but John continued his great form and went on to win the tournament. Tragically, he and fellow professional Philip Strachan were killed soon after when his Jaguar XK120 collided with an army truck while travelling to a pro-am. It was a great loss of two very talented players.

Brian Twite, Peter Mills, Jimmy Martin (Sunningdale) and Tony Harman, Coombe Hill, 1953

CHAPTER 6

The Metropolitan contingent

I SPENT MOST OF MY TIME AT SUNNINGDALE TEACHING ON THE practice fairway, but often people would book me for 9 or 18 holes on the course, which I really loved. I played with quite a few interesting and famous people this way and met several Australians who came to Sunningdale while they were on business or holidaying in the UK.

I played Joe Robinson, a fine golfer from Metropolitan, who had won the Yorkshire International, John Langley, who was a member of Sunningdale and Metropolitan, and Len Nettlefold, from Tasmania and also from Metropolitan, who was one of the best left-handers we have ever seen. One day, after Len went around in 71 and I went around in 69, he asked me: 'Have you ever thought of coming to Australia?' I said I hadn't. He said: 'What do you know about Australia?' I replied that I thought it was full of bushrangers and kangaroos, and he assured me that was not quite the way it was.

A short time later, Arthur Lees called me over and said that I had been booked to coach and play for a whole week with a group of Australians who were practising for the Lucifer tournament. 'They want to play Sunningdale and they want to play with you,' he said. I was completely taken by surprise by the request as I was only an assistant to Arthur Lees, a renowned Ryder Cup player, and I had only been at Sunningdale for less than three years, but I did as I was asked. I played with the five chaps, all from The Metropolitan Golf Club. There was Harry Hey, Clive Wallace Smith, Bill Catanach, Tom Graham and

Len Nettlefold. At the end of the week, Clive Wallace Smith, with Bill Catanach by his side, said to me: 'Brian, our club is looking for a teaching professional. We'd like you to come to Melbourne to take up the position.' They gave me an application form and said I was to let them know the next morning.

Completely surprised, I went straight to see Arthur. 'We'd better go and see the manager,' he said. I was a bit hesitant about seeing the manager as last time I had applied for a job at Glasgow six months earlier, he had called me into his office and he said: 'Twite, I've cancelled your interview. And before you say anything, you are at Sunningdale, the best club in the country. When you go for a position, you're not going to a third-rate golf club. You're going to something better.'

But this time, he got out of his chair and said: 'Twite, this is the greatest opportunity you've ever had. We all, myself included, all started at the bottom of the ladder and climbed, rung by rung. I'm at the top because I'm the manager of Sunningdale. Now, as an assistant professional, you're at the bottom of the ladder and this will take you right to the very top, and you've barely started climbing. Metropolitan is the best golf course in Australia. You're very lucky, so sign the damn form and give it to me.' I signed it and he gave it to one of his girls to post that night. My golfing career has been very lucky indeed and I have never had to apply for a position.

The next morning I told Clive Wallace Smith and Harry Hey that I had accepted the position. They were delighted and said I should book my passage as soon as possible. Clive gave me a letter and said: 'If you have any problem with the visa, give this to the Australian High Commissioner.' He was one of the finest gentlemen I have ever come across. Soon after, I received a letter from Mr J. C. McIntyre, the club captain, who said I had been appointed and to come as quickly as possible.

I immediately went to the Australian High Commission. I filled in all the forms and as I handed them to the fellow behind the counter, I said to him:' I've got to be in Melbourne as soon as possible.'

'Impossible,' he said, 'Take you six months.'

I said: 'Well, I want to see the High Commissioner.'

'He's not here.'

I said: 'Well, give this to his second-in-command.' He took the letter, and told me to take a chair. It was 10.25 am. At 3.05 pm, I was ordered to counter six.

A gorgeous girl behind the counter said: 'Mr Twite, this must be your lucky day. We've found you a passage on the MV *Georgic*, leaving the Port of Liverpool in three weeks.'

What was in that letter I don't know.

Leaving England

When I left Abbeydale, they gave me a gold watch, even though I'd only been there four years. Now I was leaving Sunningdale and they also gave me a gold watch, and I had only been there three years.

The captain of Sunningdale said it was because of the service I'd given the members. 'A lot of people just become professional and go,' he said, 'but because your service to the members at Sunningdale has been so good, we wanted to do something for you.'

I was going for five years, but I was told that, if I didn't like it, I was welcome back. Sunningdale is a great golf club, very similar to Metropolitan.

Before I left England, I went home to Leziate to say goodbye to my family and friends. Word had spread about my appointment in Australia and it was in the local paper, which also mentioned that I was coming home to play a final round at King's Lynn. The club organised an exhibition match between me and my old friend Henry Hudson. I had my lowest score ever on that Sunday. I had a 63, 12 under the card. I hit the ball so far and so straight, every hole felt like a birdie hole to me. All my shots into the green went close and all my putts went in. Remember that the holes were very short and there was a lot of run in the summer months, so I expected to have at least four birdies before I even started. On that special day, however, I was on a

:DAY, AUGUST 13, 1955   5

AUSTRALIA GOLF POST FOR TWITE

A CHANCE round of golf with an Australian has gained an English assistant professional a full post at Melbourne.

Brian C. Twite, who began his golf career when 21 years of age, at Abbeydale, Sheffield, and is now at Sunningdale, was asked to play with a visitor.

They got on so well that the sequel was an offer as professional to Metropolitan golf club, Oakleigh, an exclusive club with a membership of 1,500. Twite will sail on August 23, and will spend at least five years in Australia.

It was nearly seven years ago that Twite, a native of King's Lynn, joined Harry Atkinson at Abbeydale. He made rapid progress to become one of Sheffield's best-known young professional golfers, stayed there four years, and then joined Sheffield-born Arthur Lees, Ryder Cup player, at Sunningdale.

mission and in the zone. I was so keen to show everyone at home how well I could play, and I was so excited about my future, that I couldn't have played better.

Brian with Sadie and Terry Twite by the 14th green on his last day at King's Lynn, 14 August 1955

Henry Hudson, left, with Brian after the last game at King's Lynn

Metropolitan's new pro, good-looking bachelor

From A. R. McELWAIN

LONDON. — Brian Twite, recently appointed pro. at Metropolitan Golf Club, Melbourne, expects to reach Australia in late September or early October.

In Twite, Metropolitan will get a fine golfer and teacher from Sunnydale (Surrey) which rates as the best golf club in England.

Twite has been there for three years as assistant to professional Arthur Lees. Before that he was assistant at Abbeydale Golf Club, Sheffield, another of England's top – notch clubs.

Twite is a young (28), good looking, pleasant spoken bachelor.

He was second in the North-West England assistant professionals championship in 1951, second in the Sheffield Open, also in 1951, a quarter-finalist in the 1953 Assistant Pros'. Championship, and a grand finalist in 1954.

He is a particularly good teacher. He tells me he gets no greater satisfaction out of his job than in making an average player into a good player. He's been told Metropolitan is as good a course as Sunningdale, which makes him all the keener to get at it.

A leading Sunningdale player says the club will greatly miss Twite, who is "in every department the ideal pro."

59

Sail away

I sailed for Australia on MV *Georgic* on 19 August 1955, my twenty-ninth birthday, which was significant. This was to be my biggest adventure, combining my life in golf and my life at sea. I was well prepared, ready for the challenge and determined to make the best of it. I knew I would make a great job of my new life, whatever was in store, and I had a lot of time to think about it. The trip took six weeks and I arrived on 5 October 1955.

MV Georgic

PART TWO

THE METROPOLITAN YEARS

- CHAPTER 7 -

My new life at Metropolitan

AFTER SIX LONG WEEKS AT SEA, I WAS VERY PLEASED TO BE MET at the ship by the club captain, Jack McIntyre, and the manager, John Kissling. They took me straight to the Metropolitan Golf Club for a look at the course and to show me my accommodation in the clubhouse. I felt welcome straight away and news of my arrival had received more attention than I could have ever expected.

Jack Dillon, the main golf writer of the day, wrote an article about me and included a photo of me playing golf on the *Georgic*. I felt like a celebrity. He reported that I was the first British professional imported to Victoria since 'Bud' Russell came out 25 years earlier to work at Barwon Heads. My personal and golfing history, my best scores, my Tommy Armour golf clubs, and even my height, weight, living arrangements and new wages, were all recorded in great detail.

Another newspaper, *The Argus*, also reported my arrival and that I was surprised that I had been given the job and again when I saw the course. I was quoted as saying: 'It's one of the best I have ever seen', which it was. I actually played my first round at Metro in the afternoon of the same day that the *Georgic* berthed in Port Melbourne – Wednesday, 5 October 1955.

Settling in and getting to know Metro

One of the first people I met at Metropolitan was Horace Boorer, the club professional, who I was replacing. He was very helpful, as

was Reg Judd, the professional before him, who came to meet me. I was told that Horry had resigned to set up his own sports store in Highett and was happy to prepare me for the handover. I didn't understand until much later the full story about Horry becoming a bit too 'independent', as it was described in the club's history *Sustaining their dream*. Horry also took me to Amstel Golf Club on Show Day, a week before the handover, to 'meet the boys'. Fortunately, they

BRIAN TWITE, Metropolitan Golf Club's new professional, demonstrates on the deck of the Georgic today how he kept his eye in on the voyage from England.

Metropolitan's new pro. began golf at 5

By J. M. DILLON

An Englishman who began golf at 5 arrived on the Georgic today to become professional with the Metropolitan Golf Club.

He is Brian Twite, 29, who was reared on a farm adjoining a course at King's Lyn, Norfolk.

Twite is the first British professional imported to Victoria since "Bud" Russell of Barwon Heads came out 25 years ago.

Met by club captain, C. J. McIntyre, and manager, John Kissling, Twite was taken to the club where accommodation has been provided, and he will, after easing in for a few days, take over from Horace Boorer, on September 30.

Twite, dark, 5 ft. 9½ in. and 12 st. 7 lb. is one of a family of 11, including seven sisters.

After Royal Navy service he was assistant for four years at Sheffield and for the past three years he has been assistant to the Ryder Cupper, Arthur Lees, at famous Sunningdale.

Twite is a sound player —best in competition 68 at Sunningdale, best in practice 63 at Sunningdale and the same week-end a 64 at King's Lyn — but he has concentrated on and gained a big reputation for teaching and club making.

He arrived armed with a huge set of American clubs designed by the

famous Scottish-American Tommy Armour.

At Sunningdale in summer Twite often worked from 8.45 a.m. till 9.45 p.m. seven days a week for a wage of 50/, plus 30 per cent. of the profit he made on club activities. Winter hours were 9 a.m. to 5.30 p.m.

At Metropolitan his "retainer" will be £3 a week, he will be "found" in board and accommodation and he will have control of the business at the professional's shop.

Twite has been a full member of the PGA for four years.

liked me and welcomed me as one of the wave of New Australians arriving in Melbourne at that time.

The club looked after me in every way and I had no trouble settling in. I said from the outset that I would stay for five years, whether I liked it or not. My wage rose from 50 shillings and 50 per cent of my pro shop earnings at Sunningdale to a retainer of £3 a week, board and accommodation in the clubhouse, and full control over the Metropolitan pro shop business. To help me become established, the committee lent me the money I needed to completely restock the pro shop. Horry took everything he could with him to Highett. I got busy straight away and that's all I did. I taught all day and I stayed late, often working in the workshop until 11.00 pm.

The clubhouse with caddy master's hut on the right, from the club history, Sustaining their dream

The pro shop

The biggest surprise I had when I first arrived was the state of the professional shop. It was the worst pro shop I had ever seen. It had a dirt floor, and because everyone left food in their golf bags, it was

The pro shop in the 1950s from Sustaining their dream

rife with rats. I remembered my old boss, Harold Atkinson, saying: 'If you ever get a position, Brian, and the committee tells you that they are going to build a new shop in three years, multiply it by five and that will be about right.' And it was. It was just an old wooden shed between the 18th and the first hole. The buggy shed had a sand floor and there were no floorboards at all. We had a small workshop in which I could make whatever the members wanted, and an area to display golf equipment and clothes. I always selected the clothes myself. I bought a lot of clubs, bags, shirts and especially twin-sets from England. A matching jumper and cardigan, a twin-set was about the most important thing a woman could wear in the 1950s. I had an assistant pro to help in the shop and workshop and a number of caddies to train and supervise.

In 1971, the old pro shop was finally demolished and rebuilt as part of the renovated clubhouse. This was a great improvement.

The new pro shop and clubhouse of the 1970s, from Sustaining their dream.

The course

The course was completely different then. It was magnificent. It was kept like a botanic garden, not a weed or plant out of place. The plantations were abundant and you could not see one fairway from the other; every fairway was enclosed. We had fewer members then, perhaps only 150 playing each week, whereas now we have 650 playing weekly, so they did have to open it up a bit to allow people to find their balls and get around in a reasonable time.

To me, I'm not so happy to see the current trend where fairways have been opened up to enable you to see multiple fairways and greens at once. Still, you have to accept change and know that Metropolitan will always be a magnificent course. The quality of fairways underfoot has always been the best. Other courses have caught up, but ours have stayed the best.

The beauty of Metropolitan also has been in her signature bunkers which are cut right into the greens, so even a great shot on to the green can still roll into the sand. This is what makes the course so difficult to score on. It wasn't until Kel Nagle won a PGA here in 1967, with a four-round total of 277, that Gene Sarazen's 282 in 1936 was broken or equalled – and they were playing with old balls in those days. Jack Newton won the Australian Open in 1979 with 287.

The staff

The staff were very welcoming. I had all my meals at the club when I lived upstairs. I remember some of the long-serving characters, like Dot Jacobson in the dining room and Michael Foley and Alec Wilson in the bar.

As with the English clubs, the members were always addressed by their formal names, Mr so and so and Mrs or Miss so and so. The staff were addressed by their surname, so I was called 'Twite'. It's so different today, where everybody is equal. In England, and for the first 15 or 20 years that I was in Australia, you were a servant of the golf club. The members wanted to be up there, and you had to be down there. I had been well trained, particularly at Sunningdale, and I knew my place.

Brian with Dot Jacobson and Michael Foley receiving 25-year service watches in 1980

All the staff in those days were magnificent and we had so few compared to today.

For years we only had a manager and only one person in the office, Fay. In fact, Fay was 'the office' in those days. In the bar, Alec was magnificent. He knew exactly what members liked to drink, and how much they could drink, and he'd tell quite a few members when they had had enough and should go home.

Learning to drive

I had never learnt to drive a car and never really had to. I had always lived in the clubhouse or near the course and spent most of my time on the course. Several members, among them Bill Browning, John Donges and David Colquhoun, decided that the time had come and organised to teach me to drive on the course. I am not sure whose idea it was, but it was Bill Browning's Morris Minor, and they got me behind the wheel on the first fairway one evening after 7.00 pm.

Amid a lot of directions and laughter, I hit the accelerator instead of the brake and drove straight into the lateral fairway bunker on the right side of the first. Bill Podesta, the greens keeper, had to haul the car out very early the next morning with a tractor. Despite this drama, my lessons on the course continued and six weeks later I got my licence and bought a car.

Playing golf with the members

While I was used to playing rounds with the members at Sunningdale, I was surprised that many of the Metropolitan members drank a lot on the course, too. I played regularly with Talbot Coate, Dick Swanson and Ted Cornish. They would drink a bottle of whisky between them all the way around the golf course.

On one particular day, we were playing the 6th hole which runs alongside Huntingdale, when the boys realised they didn't have any whisky. Swanson said gruffly: 'Well, we can't play without whisky. We'll go across to Huntingdale.'

The only thing between Huntingdale and Metro was a wire fence which was only a foot high. We walked across and had three or four whiskies at the bar. This was exceptional for me because, as a professional, I could play with the members but not go into the clubhouse to have a drink with them afterwards.

We came back to Metro and finished the game and were met on the 18th by the manager, Jack Kissling. 'Brian, did you go across to Huntingdale?' he asked. I told him I had and he turned and asked Talbot what had transpired. 'Well, Kissling,' said Talbot, 'at the meeting a month ago you said we've got to be friends with Huntingdale so all we were doing was being friendly.' Everybody laughed but we were told not to do it again. It's much stricter today. The courses are fully fenced and nobody can get out or in on a normal day.

I got on so well with the members that, before long, they would invite me into the clubhouse to have a drink with them after the round on a Sunday. This was a first for Metropolitan and was followed some years later in 1967 with an Honorary Membership so that I could have a drink with the members I played with any day of the week, or come into the clubhouse to have a drink or lunch at any time by myself. I was more than happy to accompany the members, but I never went into the clubhouse without an invitation. I could never take advantage of this privilege. I just didn't feel comfortable.

While I always knew my place and would not venture my opinion unless I was asked, I always made sure I was respected. For example, I was playing in a group with Dr Guy Springthorpe one day. There were three balls already on the green and before I hit off, the good doctor said: 'I've never seen four balls on the green at the same time.'

I thought: 'The old bugger, he's trying to mozz me.' I teed up and went through the whole system that I used as a professional player in 1955 when I was playing my best golf. Of course, I hit a magnificent shot which went in the hole for one! When he looked at me, I said to him: 'You know, doctor, you're absolutely right. There aren't four balls on this green.'

Dr Springthorpe was a wonderful fellow. I enjoyed playing with him and the other guys, but I made sure they never got on top of me. I gave them just as good as they gave me and that's why I think I got along with them so well.

Among my many rounds, I recall vividly recall the time I played with young Robert Sinclair against his surgeon father, Geoff (later club captain from 1996 to 1998) and the great Glynn O'Collins (multiple club champion and senior champion between 1970 and 2000).

It should have been a win for the doctors as they started the 16th two up, and O'Collins carded an exceptional 4, 4, 3 for the final holes. But the medicos suffered 'open-course surgery' (as club historian Weston Bate called it in *Sustaining their dream*) as I birdied 16 and 17 then holed out with a 5 iron from the fairway bunker for an eagle on the last.

I used to play every Friday after work with a group of members, too. Some of the regulars were Graham Brasch (captain 1975-77), David Colquhoun, Philip Pleasance, David Ellis and John Donges.

We'd play ad hoc golf. Agreement would be made at a certain tee to play to an unrelated, distant green, and its par could be nominated as anything between three and six. On one occasion, I nominated a par seven to be played from the first tee to the 18th green at Huntingdale. I birdied it. I played my second short of the first green, my third over the majestic plantations to the third fairway, my fourth to the fifth fairway and then, after a great pitch over the trees, I sank the putt.

I also enjoyed coaching and playing with the younger members, and I still enjoy being involved in their development. I used to take a group of juniors and caddies out on the ad hoc course at the end of the day when the course was deserted. Sometimes I would let them take out only one club; I taught the caddies this way too. We all loved it.

I kept track of my own golf from the beginning by keeping an eclectic score. Over the years, I birdied and eagled nearly every hole on the course, I even had an albatross on four, which was a great thrill, with a 4 iron into the hole. There were holes-in-one on 11 with a 7 iron and on 13 with a 3 iron.

Overall, I have had six holes-in-one. My first was at King's Lynn with a 7 iron on the 12th. The next was on the Old Course at Sunningdale with an 8 iron on the 4th hole. I also had two at Rosebud Golf Club – a 5 wood on the 13th and a 9 iron on the 4th, and two at Metro.

Brian Twite's Eclectic Card

PLAYER: *BRIAN TWITE*   DATE: *1955–1994*

Hole	1	2	3	4	5	6	7	8	9	OUT
Metres	380	138	387	438	355	464	201	476	404	3243
Par	4	3	4	5	4	5	3	5	4	37
	2	2	3	2	2	3	2	3	2	21

10	11	12	13	14	15	16	17	18	IN	TOTAL
427	154	348	180	468	427	319	393	395	3111	6354
4	3	4	3	5	4	4	4	4	35	72
3	1	2	1	3	3	2	2	2	19	40

From the Club newsletter, 1994

Playing tournament golf

Although I was employed for my teaching rather than my golfing ability, I was encouraged to play in all the local professional tournaments held in Melbourne. The PGA actually waived the rules to let me play in my first tournament, the Pelaco tournament at Commonwealth, which was just a few weeks after I arrived.

It was a wonderful introduction that allowed me to put faces to the names of the top professionals and amateurs of the day. The line-up often included Peter Thomson, Kel Nagle, Ossie Pickworth, Norman Von Nida, whom I already knew from Sunningdale, and Frank Philips. Talented local amateurs included Barry West, Eric Routley and Bill Edgar.

It was a tournament of firsts, not just for me. It was played over an epic 90 holes, comprising five rounds, one round per day, with the 24 leaders playing 36 holes on the final Saturday. I qualified and played in the final. It was also Australia's first merchandising tournament with many of the players wearing Pelaco shirts.

I did much better at the next tournament at Rossdale. I came equal second with a total score of one under. I can't remember how much I won, but first prize was £1000. A few months later I played in the Speedo tournament at Victoria. Bruce Crampton was the favourite, having just won the Australian Open. He was taking on Peter Thomson and the usual line-up. I was getting to know them. That week I played with Kel Nagle and Brian Huxtable and met Doug Bachli, the British amateur champion and Victoria Golf Club member. Bruce Crampton, who turned 21 during the tournament, went on to win with a brilliant round of eight under, three under the course record.

In 1961, I met one of golf's greatest who became a lifelong friend, Gary Player. We were both playing the Ampol tournament at Yarra Yarra. It was Gary's first tournament in Australia with a prize of £10,000. He won another 10 tournaments here, including six Australian Opens and two Australian Masters. These were wonderful years.

In those days, everything was reported in the newspapers. Even a social four-ball best-ball event – an early version of a pro am – was reported. One year, I remember the Governor, Sir Dallas Brooks, and Ossie Pickworth (Royal Melbourne and later Cranbourne) won the team event with seven up, and I tied with Ossie for the best individual score of five under at Kingswood.

I loved playing in the tournaments where I made so many good friendships – Jack Harris (Albert Park), Peter Mills (Kingswood), John Clark (Long Island), Denis Denehy (Victoria), Ted Naismith (East Malvern), Noel Smith (Long Island), Robert Brown (Bendigo), Peter Block (Rossdale), John Sullivan (Sydney), John Greenhill (Western Australia), Ray Wright (Woodlands), Horace Boorer and his brother Len Boorer (Anglesea), Robbie Jamieson (Patterson River), Jack Beazley (Kingswood), Harold Knight (Southern), Geoff Flanagan (Huntingdale), Stan McGeorge (La Trobe) and Bill Clifford (Peninsula). Many of these players would become great teachers and, over the years, I played and taught alongside them and many others on many occasions.

I had some success in these tournaments, too. In April 1956, I came second to Peter Mills at Rossdale. I could have won, which would have created quite an upset. I only needed a par three on the final hole, but I sliced my tee shot, had an unplayable lie in the bushes and ran up a six.

I had more success in the foursomes. I was paired with a young John Sullivan, from Sydney, in the State Professional Foursomes in 1957. We didn't know each other, or the course, but we couldn't do a thing wrong in the final round. We won by three strokes from the Greenacres pair Viv Billings and a future Metro member, Ken Loy, with rounds at Medway of 73 and 70. The next year I played with

'Strangers' win at first try

By BILL FLEMING

BRIAN TWITE, former English professional, and John Sullivan, of Sydney, played for the first time at Medway Golf Club's course yesterday.

They took a while to settle down, but they ended up winning the State professional foursomes championship.

Twite and Sullivan won comfortably by three strokes from V. Billings and K. Loy, and N. Smith and J. Penn, 146, who tied for second place.

Leaders after the first 18, N. Smith and J. Penn, both of Rossdale, led the field with 72. Twite and Sullivan, with 73, could have improved on those figures but for erratic putting.

But after lunch the winning pair settled down to serious golf, and were never off the green under two, and with birdies at the 14th and 16th, coasted home to win the Victorian title.

Brian Twite gave credit for the win to his 22-year-old partner John Sullivan.

"He never did a thing wrong all day, and is really going places fast," he said after the match.

"We knew at the 13th that we had it in the bag, and it was a great moral booster for both of us. I have never seen Medway before, but, like all your Australian courses, it is tops," Brian said.

ASSOCIATES GOLF

CROYDON: Mrs. J. Goff (18), 2s. Second Drive: Miss U. Logan (13¼), 34½. Long Drive: Mrs. J. Goff.
KEW: Mr. H. R. Zwar (24), on count back from Miss A. Hart (22), 71. B Div.: Mrs. E. Shaw (26), 71.
KINGSTON HEATH: Mrs. R. Godfrey-Mrs. D. Rutter (33), 65. Gross: Mrs. H. Rodgers-Mrs. D. McCalman, 81.
KINGSWOOD: Mrs. C. Dowsett-Mrs. R. Smith, 86. Nett: Miss M. Mathieson-Miss D. Frost, 67.
PENINSULA: Mrs. Tracey (20)-Mrs. Aikman (24), 50.

Law list for Today

SUPREME COURT: Civil Juries: Eighth: Mr. Justice Dean: 10.30: Vincent and anor. v. Wilson and ors.; Verde v Shearer and anor.; Waddell v. Ware. Fifth: Mr. Justice Hudson: 10.30: Knowles v. Holloway (part heard): Carman v. Finkelstein; Ourrie v. Kittle and

Professional Brian Twite hits off the 4th tee at Medway yesterday. Twite and his partner John Sullivan, won the Victorian Professional championship.

John Greenhill, who later become a trainee of mine.

I soon realised that I couldn't play and teach. A reporter, Dave Andersen of *The Argus*, wrote up my dilemma in an article in June 1956. I must have mentioned to him that I didn't have enough time to complete the repairs and run the pro shop, teach all day, and then practice my own game to play in tournaments.

I really did have to decide whether to continue as a club pro and a tournament player or confine my golf interests to Metropolitan.

The reporter dramatised my situation saying: 'Englishman Brian Twite, Metropolitan's new club professional golfer, hasn't had a day off for nine months. But his doctor says that is going to stop. "I must have a day off. The doctor has warned me to eat regularly and to take at least one day a week off from golf."'

Even Jack Kissling, Metropolitan's manager, was quoted as

saying that: 'Brian has become most popular with our club. We are indeed pleased with him as professional but would like to see him take his normal time off from golf.' It was written in a humorous way, with Ossie Pickworth, chairman of the PGA, chiming in to say: 'I haven't had a day off from golf in 20 years.'

The long hours became a way of life rather than a problem for me, as it is for all professionals. I handled it by accepting it. I was doing the job I loved and happily gave my best efforts to teaching ahead of playing golf professionally. I still played in all the professional tournaments held at Metro, as was the custom, and never missed a Victorian Open when we were hosting. It was the right choice then and has always been the right choice for Metropolitan and for me.

I devoted myself to the club and its membership. I found it easy to get on with everyone, to always be courteous and patient, and I took pride in managing the more challenging members as well. I had always been taught never to say a bad word about anyone and this paid off.

I always knew my place, too. Although I had some independence in terms of running the pro shop, I was still a member of staff and a servant of the club. I had the most cordial relationship with captains and managers. There were no arguments because I was independent. I ran the shop, the manager ran the club and the captain was in control. You will find that in any golf club where the captain, the manager and the professional are all aligned the club will be a happy one, and ours was the happiest. There was always something happening, for example, Jack Kissling and member Tony Charlton even organised to promote the 1956 Melbourne Olympics from Metropolitan.

Jack Kissling, left, recording an interview with Tony Charlton, broadcast to USA Monitor program, October 1956, publicising the Melbourne Olympic Games, Brian Twite in background

– CHAPTER 8 –

Becoming a family man

IN THOSE FIRST FEW YEARS, I DIDN'T HAVE MUCH TIME TO MAKE friends and socialise away from golf. I lived in the clubhouse for two years and then moved to a unit on Warrigal Road, South Oakleigh. As I as working seven days a week, there wasn't time to go out but I didn't mind.

I met Shirley Isobel Ramsay in 1955 when I first came to Metropolitan. Shirley worked in the dining room. I used to come across to the clubhouse for lunch every day and Shirley, who was a gorgeous girl, would have my lunch ready for me. We always chatted but there was no thought of going out with her at all until one of the girls in the kitchen suggested I should take Shirley out for dinner. It went on from there.

I knew Shirley for nearly four years before we were married on 21 August 1958. We were married at St John's Church, in Toorak, by Caroline Nicholson's father, Canon Russell Clark, who was a clerical member at Metro and a good friend.

I had planned to play in the Australian Open with Gary Player that year, but cancelled when we decided to get married. Instead, we drove to Adelaide for our honeymoon and saw Gary win the Australian Open at Kooyonga Golf Club.

My holidays and all my family milestones can be linked to attending a major golf tournament.

We came home via the coast road and stayed at Apollo Bay. We only had one upset during the whole trip. It was very wet and the car got so bogged in Apollo Bay we had to get a tow truck the next morning to get us out.

We came home and soon after bought a house in Huntingdale, at 17 Jason Street. We lived there until our house on Golf Road was completed in 1962.

Our daughter, Sadie Ann, was born on 23 May 1959. I was teaching one Saturday and I got a phone call at about 10.00 am to say that the baby had been born. I went straight away to the hospital to see her. We named her after my youngest sister.

We adjusted to our new lives. I was kept working seven days a week while Shirley, a devoted mum, stayed home and looked after the baby. It was just part and parcel of family life in those times.

Two years later, our second daughter, Susan, arrived on 22 June 1961. Shirley loved the name and we called her Susie. She was a very good baby too; all our children were very good. Andrew arrived three and a half years later on 22 December 1964. Shirley was thrilled as she really wanted a son. We were so fortunate to have two girls and a boy.

Building the family home on the 17th

The golf course went through some major changes in the 1950s. The suburbs were spreading out and as land prices rose, our neighbouring market gardens, which formed a wedge through the middle of the course, became ripe for housing subdivision.

Our council rates were going up to fund the new roads and services, and the Education Department was looking at land in Oakleigh for two new schools to support the population increase. Metropolitan and Huntingdale golf courses were also seen as potential sites for the new Monash University, and survival of both courses was at stake.

As a result of some complicated land deals, the Metro committee bought two market gardens and sold a parcel to the Education Department, which included the original 13th and 14th. It then subdivided and sold the old 17th along Golf Road, and the land fronting North Road and Voumand Street.

We lost three holes but they were replaced by holes designed by Dick Wilson and this saved the course.

An Act of Parliament brought in by the Victorian Premier, Sir Henry Bolte and his Attorney-General, Arthur Rylah, saw Metropolitan, Huntingdale and Spring Valley golf clubs declared protected as a green belt. Later, Commonwealth Golf Club was added to the group. Our boundaries were consolidated to form a rectangle.

When the subdivided parts of the course went up for sale, Mr Kissling came into the pro shop asked me if I wanted to buy a piece of the land. I said yes, and he told me I could have whatever block I wanted.

I chose the last block, 14 Golf Road, on the 17th, which was nearest to the clubhouse. It was perfect. Most of the plots were sold for £2000. We paid £1750, and the Club gave me an interest-free loan for 10 years. It was excellent.

We were fortunate also to have the architect Ian Turner, a Metro member, design and build our house. We didn't like his first design, which had a flat roof. We really wanted a nice English-style house with a pitched roof, and he did that for us. We moved into our dream home in 1962.

In those days, people, particularly the men, didn't play as well as they do today. They would often hook their shots into the 17th

'Brian is outstanding for his personal integrity. He set a standard of behaviour amongst the pros and expected that standard of behaviour from members too. He never criticises them when they fall short of it but had his own private opinion about it. He has affected the ethos of the club by his own personal values which he spread around where ever he was, and people assimilated that, and it's part of the ethos of Metro, that's my personal opinion.'

Bill Kimber, friend and Metro member

green, sometimes very badly. Regrettably, these stray balls would land on our roof, and we wouldn't always know until it rained.

Jack Kissling would send someone down to repair it. The Club, of course, paid for all the windows and roof tiles that were broken, but it was still awful.

One day, Shirley was having a shower and a ball came through the bathroom window and into the shower. She rang me up, frightened that someone was throwing bricks at the house. I rushed home and found a golf ball in the shower. I knew who it was, as I had just seen him walking away from the house looking for a ball. When I got back to the clubhouse, I returned the ball to him. 'Where did you find this, Brian?' he asked. 'In my shower!' I replied.

In later years, when the original fence wore out and we no longer had a fence, I would often be sitting in the garden with a cup of coffee on a Saturday afternoon before going back to work and suddenly a ball would come on to the lawn. Of course, it was out of bounds and the guy would come up and give it a kick back on the course. Quite often I'd see the same fellow back at the shop and ask him what he had on 17. He might say a five and I'd say: 'Five and a free kick.' You couldn't really say any more than that or they would be disqualified.

Life was easy then and the times were good. There were not the crimes or the drugs or the pressures there are today for youngsters. It was just normal, peaceful living.

Brian looking out over the 17th from 14 Golf Road, Oakleigh South

The kids didn't have far to walk to the new South Oakleigh Primary School, which was built behind the 17th tee, or the Huntingdale High School (now the primary school) which was built behind the sixth green.

They liked living on the course, too. Sadie Ann was obsessed with horses and National Velvet for years. She could never understand why we had all the land behind us yet we didn't have horses. She wanted me to buy one for her and put it on the course where it could roam freely and drink from the dam. To compensate, she played with imaginary horses by tying a rope between two trees in the backyard. Some of the members would be amused and tell me that they had seen Sadie Ann riding her horse again. Later, all three children rode real horses with mixed success.

We managed the three kids well, primarily because Shirley was an excellent mother. I probably didn't spend as much time with them over the weekend as I should have, but that's what happens when you're working every day. All the professionals worked six or seven days a week in those days. Shirley didn't mind. She might occasionally

'There was always golfing memorabilia around the house and on the walls, and golf shoes and odd clubs at the front door. We had golf balls on the roof and coming through the windows. We'd be sitting there watching television and bang – another ball had arrived.'

Sadie Ann Heizer, daughter

complain, but she understood that we needed the money to keep the place going.

Unfortunately, Shirley was never interested in golf, while everything in my world always revolved around golf. However, she was a keen gardener. We only had a small back yard, so she had lots of indoor plants and often used old golf sticks in the pots to support them. Our friends and visitors would often be surprised to see the head of a four wood in the middle of a pot plant.

Teaching the kids to play

I taught all three children to play golf when they were little. Sadie Ann always had a very good swing. She was the only girl in a group of 12 boys at primary school who played golf on a Wednesday afternoon at East Malvern public golf course. The teacher would say: 'Who wants to play with Sadie Ann?' and no-one did. So the teacher asked her to have a shot and when she put it straight on the green, every kid wanted to play with her. She played until other interests took over.

Susie played too but wasn't suited to it – she always thought it was too far to walk. She did play at times and still enjoys golf as a social game.

Andrew took it up more seriously, and he was really good. He could have been brilliant; he could even have become a professional. When he was fifteen, he could hit a ball off the 18th tee at Metro and be only 50 metres short of the green. He would be there time after

Holiday photos with Shirley, Brian, Sadie Ann, Susie and Andrew, circa 1970

time. We played together four years ago at Indooroopilly. He is still a massive hitter, but sadly not always in the right direction.

Family holidays

For years I took the family to Lakes Entrance for the Christmas school holidays and then further on to Merimbula. Our biggest family trip was in 1969 when I took everyone home to Leziate to see my parents for their Golden Wedding anniversary. We had had a telegram earlier to say Dad was dying, and at the same time he got our letter saying we were coming to visit in August. Dad was so pleased to get this news that he got out of bed, got into the Guinness and said: 'I'm not going to die until they come home.' He lived for another 12 months.

We had a big shindig at the village hall and the whole family came from everywhere across the world to be there. I remember Andrew had an asthma attack in Grantham and went to hospital which was frightening, but otherwise it was a wonderful trip. Our visit was even reported in the newspaper.

'We were mostly treated as celebrities, but Dad's mother was very matter-of-fact about us. She was quite a stoic woman, and she ruled the house with an iron fist. I remember visiting King's Lynn and the house in Council Road, and we mistakenly walked in with our shoes on. We were told to back out and take our shoes off before ever coming in again. We were also introduced to Horlicks and the routine of having an early "tea", followed by "supper", a later meal at about 8.00 pm.'

Sadie Ann Heizer, daughter

Sylvia and William Twite, circa 1980

Losing Shirley and managing the kids

Our family life changed forever when Shirley died suddenly at home of a massive asthma attack eight days before Christmas on 17 December 1971. Sadie Ann and Susie were with her and had already called Dr Peace, who had attended briefly and gave her a needle before heading off, saying she would be fine. But she wasn't, and she started going blue. Sadie Ann was remarkable. She rang the doctor again, but he hung up on her, so she rang me. She finally got through to the doctor, and then to an ambulance and then to me. We were all there together, but it was too late. She choked and died. Shirley was only 33 and our

AUSTRALIAN GOLFER RETURNS TO LYNN

'From the beginning, Dad gave us that sense that, even though it was devastating, we had to keep going with that traditional English stiff upper lip approach which was very much a part of who he was. I think we all rallied behind that. I remember we all walked up to the local shopping centre where you had your greengrocer, butcher and chemist in those days. I remember going in the fruit shop a few days after. Joe the fruiterer was in tears. We took the emotion on board, we just had to continue on. It affected me later and still does. But Dad definitely held it together.'

Sadie Ann Heizer, daughter

kids were only twelve, ten and seven.

It was difficult. It had a huge impact on us all, but you accepted it because you'd seen people die the in the war. It was just one of those things. It just happened, and that was all there was to it.

The girls took it very well, at the time at least. Only Andrew couldn't accept it and he didn't accept it for years. He needed her. Of course, children need their mother at that age. Fathers can work seven days a week, twelve hours a day, but Mum has to be there for 24 hours a day. She's always there. It was really hard.

'Mum used to teach me how to do things and I always used to ask because I was always interested. I was already capable when she passed away, so I took over the cooking and cleaning. Even straight away, it was eight days before Christmas and I still did the Christmas turkey, ham and all the vegetables. I did the whole Christmas dinner because I knew how to cook everything.'

Susie Gracey, daughter

I had to change the system a bit and rearrange my times. Instead of starting work at 7.00 am, I came in at 9.00 am after I'd taken the kids to school. The kids all went to South Oakleigh Primary School which was then behind the 17th so they could walk. Later, the girls went to Huntingdale High School which was behind the sixth hole. They looked after themselves after school and the girls would cook dinner.

My mother and my sister Wendy came from Leziate as soon as they could. But it didn't work out as hoped.

The girls were terrific. They did all the cooking and when I got home, the meal was always there. It didn't matter what it was or whether it came out of a tin or was meat pies and all those sorts of things. After 12 months, they became very good cooks. Sadie Ann

'Grandma and Aunty Wendy arrived three months after Mum died and that's when the fun and games started. We had just got our routine sorted but they were from a different era and we couldn't cope too well. Grandma was a woman who would rule us with her iron fist. I can still remember the awful smell of kippers being cooked in the morning. Mum's mother, Marie, also came to help but she was getting on and was already very busy looking after six foster children. They all had their own ideas and I don't think it worked with Marie either. Mum's sister, Lorraine, would pop in for a visit from time to time, so we really did learn how to do it on our own.'

Sadie Ann Heizer, daughter

certainly did. She did everything by the book. Susie didn't. She just put this in and that in, and her cakes were always better than Sadie Ann's.

We managed very well together over the next eight years. The kids went through school as far as they wanted to go, and mostly looked after themselves at the weekend. The girls finished their time at Huntingdale High School, while Andrew went to Mentone Grammar. They were adventurous as teenagers. Sadie Ann became obsessed with surfing and I would stop my lessons on Saturday afternoons and take her to Phillip Island after I discovered that she had been hitchhiking there with a girlfriend. The girls remember me taking them to concerts at Festival Hall to see the likes of Suzi Quatro and Cat Stevens, and that I had to wait for them in the car with Andrew, and then find them afterwards.

Andrew played in local cricket and football teams and it was a great help when Sadie Ann got her licence and she could drive them around in her little Volkswagen Beetle.

Susie was first to start work when she was just fourteen and a half years old. She was interested in hairdressing, so I sent her to a

'Sadie Ann nearly poisoned us quite a few times. She'd take steak out in the morning, thaw it out, then change her mind, pop it back in the freezer and take out fish. After a few upset tummies, she learnt she couldn't do that anymore.'

Susie Gracey, daughter

hairdressing chap I had given lessons to and he got her a job in Chapel Street, Prahran. She loved it and stayed in hairdressing for 20 years. Sadie Ann became a nanny to the one family for five years and she loved that. Andrew went to Queensland when he was seventeen or eighteen and liked it so much he stayed there.

Dad was an awesome dad and one of his best dad moments that I can remember involved my cricket bat. He used to drop me off at the school bus stop every morning and on one particular morning he discovered that I had left my bat in the back of the car. I realised this when the bus was a couple of stops up the road. Dad must have chased after the bus, because next I see him getting out of his car, jumping on the bus and making his way down to the back – I was one of those cool kids – to give me my cricket bat.

As a teenager I was a bit embarrassed, but it didn't impact me much at the time. Now that I'm older, and wiser and have my own family, I can see it what a really awesome gesture it was. It was such a part of who Dad was. He was willing to go to any lengths, to do everything he possibly could do, for me and my sisters to fill the gap left when Mum died. And he did. I appreciate him now also as an awesome grandfather. He never forgets a birthday and my kids and wife just love him too.'

Andrew Twite, son

CHAPTER 9

Running the Pro Shop

Clubmaking

It wasn't my main focus, but we did make a lot of clubs in the early years at Metro. We had a shed with sand on the floor for storing the golf clubs and all the buggies. We also had a workshop with all the club-making facilities we needed.

Source: Club newsletter 1994

It wasn't hard to make the clubs – it just took a lot of time – or to fit them to people. You just looked at the person and you knew how strong they were. You knew what shots they wanted. You knew the fingers or grip you needed, and I made a lot of clubs this way. The men's and the ladies' clubs we made were different, as the heads of the ladies' woods and irons were always lighter than the men's.

Some of the members were more of a challenge, however. One day, Bill Priestley, who was on the committee and stood 6 foot 4 inches tall and built like a two iron, came in to the shop. 'Twite, I want a new set of woods. I want a driver, a spoon (three wood) and a baffy (rescue wood).' So I made them. It took me three weeks to make the heads from wooden blocks. I stained them maroon red and they were beautiful.

He took them out, came back, and said: 'This is the worst bloody set of clubs I've ever had. Now if you can't make them better, make me a new set.' I said to my staff in the shop: 'All right, scrape them down.' We scraped them down, painted them again and, this time, we stained them black. I gave them to him the week after.

He took them out. 'That's the finest set of clubs I've ever had, Twite,' he said.

Funnily enough, a highly polished wood in black always looks smarter than a red head. Why that is I have no idea, but you can put two identical clubs together, a red one and a black one, and the black one always looks better.

In 1957 or 1958 Dunlop started making their own wooden heads and all you did was buy the heads and put them on steel shafts. By

the early 1960s, golf factories were making all the heads and you could just buy them. Instead of taking three of four weeks, it took only three of four days to assemble a club because you'd simply choose a head, select a shaft, put it in and

then stain and polish the head and put the transfer 'Brian Twite' on the top of it.

After a while, manufacturers did everything for me, including putting my name on the top of the woods and stamping it on the sole of the irons. I used to order 200 Pin Splitter and Pin Pointer clubs from Scotland every year, made by the club manufacturer George Nichol, with Henry Cotton's name stamped on them. Interestingly, in UK and later in Australia, the more expensive, top-grade clubs bore the names of famous players like Gary Player, but in the United States, the cheaper clubs had a professional's name on them.

The last club I made was for Dr Guy Springthorpe. He had a baffy, which is like a rescue club. He broke it and I made him a new baffy out of a driver block. The head was magnificent. It was about three inches long and an inch high and three inches wide; a beautiful club. We also bought putter heads and just had to put shafts on them. I remember when Bill Edgar was in charge of the Golf Foundation 50 years ago, we made dozens of putters out of two irons. We just put a putter shaft in and some of them were beautiful putters.

By the 1980s, we were no longer making clubs at all. While we can still put new shafts into every club that breaks, most clubs today are guaranteed for one or two years, so they are simply sent back to the manufacturer.

I continued to adapt clubs to suit changing needs, whether it was some extra weight in the head for greater feel, or to modify a slice or changing the length or lie of the club. I still love tinkering with clubs in my garage.

It was always a pleasure to help the greats, too. When Arnold Palmer came to Australia he would bring ten wedges with him. After playing the course, he would come into the pro shop and say: 'Brian, do you mind if I borrow a dust jacket and do some work on my clubs?' He would put his wedges in the vice and grind them to the right bounce. I would leave him to it. He didn't want anyone to touch the clubs; he wanted to do all the work himself.

Another time, though, he did let me adjust his putter. Arnold wanted it to be a bit flatter because our greens were so fast. So we went out the back to my repair bench and put the putter in the vice. I took a bit of four-by-two and gave it a whack in just the right place. He almost fell over but recovered quickly. He took it out of the vice, put it on the ground, looked at it and announced: 'It's exactly what I wanted. How the hell did you do that?' 'By instinct,' I replied.

Staffing the pro shop

When I first started at Metropolitan, the only person helping me in the pro shop was Phillip, the trainee assistant I inherited. He had hair about 4 feet long and I told him if he didn't cut it he could leave. He said: 'I'm not gonna cut it.' So he left.

Then I employed John Greenhill, from Western Australia, as a trainee pro. He's the father of David Greenhill who's now at Golf Victoria. John was with me for four years before I got him a job at the Claremont Golf Club, in Tasmania. He was there for 25 years. One of the television networks put him on an episode of This *is Your Life*. Then John came back to Victoria and worked at Peninsula, then Spring Valley and finally Huntingdale. Following him, his son David continues to be a great force in Victorian golf administration. I have remained friends with the whole family over the years.

Other trainees I worked with included Lee Wasle, Peter Crouch, Cameron Wade, Gary Davis, and his brother Paul Davis, who has been the professional at the Coolangatta and Tweed Heads Golf

John Greenhill with Brian after winning the Victorian Foursomes Championship at Kew in 1958

Club, in Queensland, for the last 30 years. He's done really well. Also, John Furze, Ivan Campbell, Struan McDowall and Trevor Pridmore, who went to Morack Golf Course, in Vermont South. One of the caddies, Brian Reiter, also became a trainee. Tim Silver was the main one and he stayed with me for six years. He became the professional at Oakleigh Golf Course for about 29 years, and then he went down to Rosebud Country Club, the Rosebud public course, and he was there for many years. Another one I remember was Graham Hoskins. He was a very good player and was with me for four years before he left to run his own shop as a professional at Waverley Golf Club.

All my trainees either went on to other golf clubs or they played tournament golf. They all had aspirations at one time or another of going on tour. Some of them weren't good enough and some of them could have been very good players, but they had to work and pay for themselves, and of course, they just fell by the wayside. There were very few sponsors in those days.

I taught them how to be good club professionals for members and to understand the members, and some of them needed quite a lot of teaching. I found it easy to teach them how to size up people in a few minutes by watching the way they talk and the way they walk.

We have a fellow at Metro today who is a wonderful man, but he is army, and everything is army, and when you are playing with him, which I enjoy, he speaks with so much authority, you feel like one of his troops. You can pick him out in two minutes.

Many of my former trainees have recognised how valuable their time at Metro was, which I really love to hear. John Furze, who had worked at several clubs before working with me at Metro, said in a recent golf article: 'It was here that my love for teaching really took off, as I was fortunate to be under the guidance of one of Australia's most respected and sought-after teachers.'

Some stayed on after their three trainee years, but most of them went on to become professionals in other golf clubs because, like everything else, whether you are a green keeper, a chef or a professional, anybody who is from Metropolitan has a 10 per cent extra chance of getting a job before anybody else.

Metropolitan was considered number one and working for Brian Twite was number two. The same with our green keepers. They could always get jobs at other fine clubs because they had been taught correctly, and they know what they do and they are professionals at their jobs.

For these reasons, I never had to advertise. People would come around month after month, asking: 'If you have a vacancy, Mr Twite, let me know.' When I did need someone, I just had to look up my list and decide which one I wanted.

In all the years I ran the pro shop, I've only had one bad one, a young boy from another golf club who I had to sack within 12 months. I told him he could either resign or be sacked because he was stealing everything out of the shop and selling it on the weekend at the local market. I kept missing golf clubs and eventually I set a trap for him. A box of new heads come in and I said to him: 'Now I want you to look after these. Don't let anybody have these heads. These are very special.' A week after, half of them disappeared. I knew where they went. So I went to Albert Park Golf Course and there they were.

Even if someone was working at another club and I asked them to come in, they would leave their job and come to Metro. You could have people from Yarra Yarra, Kew, Green Acres, anywhere, because they all wanted to train at Metropolitan. In the 1940s, '50s and '60s, you spoke of Metro very quietly because it was, in my view, the best golf club in Australia, and it still is. Metropolitan still has a great name.

Bill Clifford, a professional from Peninsula, also worked with me. He wanted to teach at Metropolitan, which he did on Fridays when I taught in the country. He also held the fort when I later took golf tours to England for five weeks at a time.

I also had two men working for me in the pro shop on Mondays and Wednesdays, cleaning all the clubs. One was Peter Stickley, who loved working with me. He once told me that his time at Metro was one of the best times in his life.

The pro shop was mostly looked after by the trainees, while I chose the clothes and the clubs for the shop. My job was mostly giving lessons and looking after the members and the club-making was secondary. We had a caddy master to look after the caddies.

Training the caddies

We had 30 caddies when I started at Metropolitan, most of them young boys from the local neighbourhood. Buggies had been introduced, but many players still preferred to have a caddy. We had a caddy master, Jack Collins, who had a little hut in the driveway in front of the clubhouse. The members would park, pay sixpence to Jack and he would organise one of the caddies waiting nearby. The caddy would get a number and take it to the pro shop to get the player's clubs out. Jack would tell them what to do, and when they came into the shop, I'd tell them what to do.

The things I taught them were the same things Jack Lovelock and Arthur Gladman, the professional at Kings' Lynn before him, had taught me as a young caddy – you must always dress smartly, have clean shoes and get to the ball first. These were the magic rules which always worked.

I said the same to John Smith, who was aged about ten when he came here. He bravely said he didn't want to caddy for Dr Springthorpe because all the caddies had told him he was terrible. So I said to John before his first round: 'Just get to his ball first and stay there until he gets there, and you'll never have a problem.' And he didn't. After two rounds, Guy Springthorpe came to see me and said: 'Twite, that kid's a good caddy.'

In fact, Dr Springthorpe and Lionel Ferguson, who used to play together a lot, decided to help John when he left school at sixteen. The doctor said to Fergie and me in the bar one day while having a drink: 'We've got to do something for John Smith. We've got to find him a job.'

He said to Fergie, who was head of the Yorkshire Insurance Company in Melbourne: 'Now Fergie, you can give him a job sweeping the floors to start him off.' Ferguson did, and within 12 months, Fergie said to me: 'That kid will run this bloody company in five years' time.' And he did.

Because he was so respected by Dr Springthorpe and Fergie, they got him a job and that's how he came to have his own insurance company and later he became a Metropolitan member, too.

It was also important that the caddies didn't chat among themselves or complain about the people they were caddying for. If they did, they had to keep it between themselves because whatever you said always got back to the person involved. Even today, if you say something bad about somebody in a roundabout way, it gets back to that person. And it's not good. A good relationship between caddy and player must be respectful both ways. As their

'Fergie got me the job in Yorkshire Insurance Company through an ex-navy mate and guided me through the insurance industry for the next 20 years. One day, I was visiting the pro shop when Twite and Guy Springthorpe asked me if I'd like to play golf there. Guy and Lionel proposed and seconded me into Metro and I was in within a month. I had played pennant for Kingwood for about 12 years and was delighted to join Metro and play pennant with Michael Clayton, John Kelly, Michael Sammels and Clyde Boyer. Brian had taught me well, but the biggest thing was that he never tried to change my swing because he knew that it was very difficult to change a golf swing. He focused on making sure that my hands were in the right place most of the time. I'd go to him for years after that and he'd always say: "Don't listen to those people. Most of the time your hands are in the right place, just get out there and hit it." He always encouraged me to play my own game and he still does that. It's a very special and close relationship that is hard to put into words, but it's just fantastic.'

John Smith, caddy, player and Metro member

Lionel Ferguson, Guy Springthorpe and Wayne Hinton with starter John Maine, and young caddie Paul Ansell in the background

employer, the players should look after their caddies and encourage them to do the right thing.

Another thing Jack also told us was that if anything is wrong, always count to ten before you say something. If somebody says something to you that you don't like, instead of bursting out saying something back to them, you start counting and it will quieten you down. Then you can either ignore it or say something else. This has always been good advice for me.

I also used to match the caddies to the players when I could. You always put the quiet boy with the quiet member. It was easy to look at the member and think, well, he's a bit arrogant, I'll put so and so with him because he's strong enough to take it and not say anything. But the first thing they were taught was not to speak back. And that's where the counting to ten came in.

If the player didn't like the caddy, they'd come into the shop and say: 'Twite, that caddy needs a good talking to. He's lagging behind, talking to his friends.' This was the biggest fault because it meant the caddy didn't get to the ball first.

They were always given a second chance, but if they still didn't measure up, they were told to get off. Some of them would clear off by themselves. Dr Springthorpe was rude to one young caddy before John Smith's time. The caddy just left his bag on the fairway and walked off.

Another time, again before John came along, Dr Springthorpe came out one Sunday and he wanted a caddy. I said: 'There are no caddies, sir.'

'Well, go and get a caddy!' he demanded.

I said: 'Well, I've got a girl who will caddy for you, if you promise not to swear. She's on a one handicap. Her name's Ann Joyce and she is a lovely girl.'

He agreed not to swear and all was fine until the bunker on the second. The first shot didn't come out. The second shot didn't come out. When the third didn't come out, he let go.

Ann said to him: 'That's all right, I'm from the country and I've heard worse than that.'

At the end of the round, he gave her double the usual rate which was $5 a round. It's the only time a girl has ever caddied because it was an emergency. Ann loved it and would have done it again, but girls just didn't caddy in those days. Quite a few of the ladies had caddies. I remember Do (Dorothy) Lonie, who was captain at one time, and later president, and Joan Dixon, also a captain and a club champion, quite often had a caddy.

We had some very good caddies who became very good golfers. The Reiter brothers, who lived on North Road, for example, were all extremely good, with Alan and Don both going on to win Victorian Amateur Championships. Alan also won several Victorian and Australian Schoolboy Championships. Their father, Keith, was a great player too. His idea was to get them on the golf course playing golf instead of getting into trouble. As boys, they did nothing else. They would hit more than 2000 balls a week between them on the practice fairway and they were allowed to play on the course before 9.00 am and after 4.00 pm. They played on the course night after night after night. Often in the summer after work, I would go out and play five or six holes with them.

'Brian was fantastic. He was never short of giving his time, or anything else we needed, to all the caddies who wanted to play the game, and there were about 20 of us during the 1950s. As caddies, we were part of his extended family and he treated us so well. I remember as a nine-year-old kid, I was left-handed and he said to me: 'What hand do you write with, son?' I said right-handed. He took the two left-handed clubs off me and gave me three right-handed clubs and said: 'You are right-handed from this day. Whatever hand you write with, that's the hand you should play golf with.' He was correct, and we never doubted his authority on anything.

He was a brilliant teacher. The way he could communicate with the average golfer was exceptional, and that's why he is still giving lessons at Metropolitan today. 'Twitey' could get ordinary people to play well and enjoy their golf. He could remedy any problems and get them to do anything – a total gift to the club golfer. He could also do many things at once. He would be giving a lesson on the practice fairway, selling golf clubs to people in the pro shop and checking on someone else's swing as he walked by. Everyone loved him because he would give everybody his time.

Brian gave us our golfing upbringing based on his English upbringing. He taught us everything we needed to know to be the best caddies we could be. Everyone *had to be presentable or you didn't get to caddy. You had to have clean shoes, that was part of the deal. We had a wow of a time, but you had to behave yourself. The discipline needed to be a caddy was high, and that was all done to Brian's standards. We were taught to be very respectful of all the members. We always called all our players 'Sir'.*

I caddied for the Victorian Governor, Sir Dallas Brooks. On many occasions, I would even wag school to caddy for him. One day I left school before lunch saying I was sick and the next morning I was on the front page of the Age with the Governor. The school couldn't do much about it, because in those days, the Governor was the truant officer. Years later, the Governor saw me at a tournament, went right across the green to shake my hand and said he remembered me. Later we also used to caddy for Sir Henry Winneke, the next Governor, and his sons.

We also caddied for the pennant team and the best players, the likes of Tom Crow, who started Cobra Golf, Peter Thomson, Doug Bachli and Billy Dunk. I was also fortunate to caddy for Jack Harris when he won the Victorian Open in 1959 at Metro and for Kel Nagle for six years, both in Victoria and interstate.'

Graeme Reiter, caddy and player

The Reiter brothers on the 5th green at Metropolitan, circa 1961. From left and in age order: Keith (father), Brian, Don, (Keith junior absent), Alan, Graeme, and Colin

Dick Kirby, Caddy Champion of Victoria, 1955, photo taken by The Sun newspaper

I also used to take the best caddies to the caddies' tournaments. I remember I took Alan Reiter to Kew one year where he had 69 and 71 to win the championship, and I took a carload to the caddies' championship at Croydon on a few occasions.

The caddies also loved being part of the big tournaments where they could watch and even caddy for some of the best players of the day. The Victorian Open was held at Metropolitan in 1960, 1975, 1978 and each year from 1980 to 1985 organised by Metro member and sports broadcaster Tony Charlton. We also hosted the Australian Open in 1979, 1986, 1993 and 1997. So we had the greatest names in golf in the pro shop – Jack Nicklaus, Arnold Palmer, Gary Player and Seve Ballesteros and local greats Peter Thomson, Kel Nagel, Bruce Devlin, David Graham and later, Greg Norman was a regular.

As keen golfers, some of the caddies not only became great golfers and went on to make significant contributions to golf. Dick Kirby also won a caddies' championship in 1955 and grew up to be President of Spring Valley, the Victorian Golf Union and the Australian Golf Society. I gave Dick a lesson just the other day and he still remembers those early times very fondly.

'I started caddying at Metro when I was 11 and I was one of the first people to meet Brian when he arrived in 1955. I knew Shirley Ramsay, too, before Brian met and married her. We were in the same class at primary school. She was a year older, extremely good looking and quite unforgettable.

I was 17 when Brian arrived, and we were a bit worried about this very 'proper' English professional we were getting from Sunningdale, but he was just a normal guy who was a really good golfer.

He started playing with, and teaching us, straight away, and he is the best teacher, and practically the only teacher, I have ever had. He taught me to work on my grip and my swing planes and things like that, and not to change my swing to something I didn't have.

If I was on the practice fairway, Brian would give me technical advice in between and even during his other lessons. After you had a lesson with Brian, which I did regularly, you could play on the course, and as I had been a caddy, I was never questioned by the ground staff.

I loved playing with Brian and the other caddies when we had the course to ourselves and could play it in new ways. We would play the back nine backwards, play the course off the ladies' tees, create new holes, say from the old 10th to the old 14th green, (the old 14th was one of the best holes ever) and even devise whole new courses.

One favourite was to start on the old 11th and play down 12, 13 and 14, climb over the fence into Commonwealth and play from 4 up to 8, then head across the paddock and climb over the fence into Yarra Yarra and play a few holes there. On the way back, we would play the 2nd and 3rd hole at Commonwealth, climb back over fence into Metro to play 15, 16 and finish on the old 17th.'

Dick Kirby, caddy, player and golf administrator

The famous Reiter brothers, Brian, Don, Keith junior, Alan, Graeme, and Colin, joined their father at Huntingdale when they were old enough, and Yarra Yarra, where they stocked their pennant teams, as well as the Victorian state team, for many years.

Sometimes, in the early years, I would have one of the caddies caddy for me. John Smith and Paul Ansell caddied for me a couple of times. Paul remembers being a very shy young caddie who would rarely talk, which would have been an asset at the time.

'I was one of seven kids and all my older brothers were caddies at Metro. While I was extremely shy, there were a few scallywags who would bet on the horses and kick a footy around. One really hot day when Brian was away and there was no one on the course, I remember a few of us and the assistants decided to go for a swim in Brian's pool. We took off the pool cover and were jumping in and splashing about when suddenly Brian turned up! We scrambled back to the pro shop as fast as we could. Brian was stern but not cross with us and there were no repercussions. We used to swim in the lake too when we could, and tadpole in the pond next to the first green.

Despite a few break outs, we were extremely well trained. The most important things we learnt were to dress smartly and to always tuck your shirt in and have clean shoes, and to keep up and all the on-course etiquette such as holding the pin correctly and standing in the right place. We worked hard but were well rewarded too. We always had pocket money, and once a year we were treated to an annual caddies' tournament with a large trophy, and were served party pies, sausage rolls and lemon squash in pewter mugs!

Brian was our mentor. He taught us everything we needed to know regarding manners and golfing skills in the old pro shop and on the course. We learnt how to clean and buff the clubs with a machine, change grips, lacquer the woods, and how to pick up balls on the practice fairway without a helmet. On the practice fairway, he taught us the fundamentals of the game and the unconventional shots such as his signature driver shot off the deck, how the bend our shots around and over trees and a few novelty shots too. In those day, there were huge trees on the first nine. All the holes and the greens were enclosed by trees then, such as the first and the second greens that you wouldn't recognise today. The fifth was so well treed there were goannas and rabbits and foxes to contend with as well as the tall trees when went cross country as Brian created new holes for us to play.

Brian was a brilliant ball-striker. I caddied for him in a few tournaments. He was so impressive to watch; and although he was so fit and powerful and could play every shot ever needed, he did get nervous. He was a better player when he was playing with members and kids and was a master of novelty shots too. He taught us the right fundamentals for each of us and would always correct us if he saw we were doing something wrong from a distance and would even interrupt a lesson to tell us. He was anti changing your natural swing, so he wasn't so popular with the next generation of elite club golfers such as Mike Clayton, John Kelly and Clyde Boyer as they sought to be the best they could be with new techniques and technology such as cameras and video recorders. He helped them where he could, but they found pros elsewhere like Geoff Parslow at Yarra.

For us though, as a role model, he gave us a fabulous grounding in golf and life. He was nurturing, respectful, confident, passionate and caring. He was a proud and honourable man who loved golf so much, he shared his love with us and taught us to love and honour the game too.'

Paul Ansell, caddy, player and Metro member

Over time the number of caddies needed became smaller and smaller until we only had a few regulars on a Saturday and Sunday. Pull buggies and electric buggies came in and instead of paying $5 for a caddy, they'd use a club buggy or buy their own. Eventually the caddies just disappeared.

– CHAPTER 10 –

My teaching career

Teaching at Metro

Between 1955 and 1965, there were three main golf pros in Melbourne – Ray Wright at Woodlands, Harold Knight from Southern, and me. People always used to say: 'Who are we going to? Knight, Wright or Twite?' I also had a little fun with words. Instead of a business card, I had a book of matches to give away with 'If your swing is not Twite Right, see Brian Twite' printed on the back.

We three did 80 per cent of all the golf teaching in Melbourne. We had a virtual monopoly, but that changed when the younger ones came up in the 1970s and 1980s, like Bruce Green at Royal Melbourne, and Geoff Flanagan and his assistant Steve Banon at Huntingdale.

Teaching all day for six days, often seven days per week, adds up to over 150,000 lessons over my 70 years of teaching. It's hard to estimate how many pupils that would involve. Mostly I have taught the club golfer who just wants to improve. I would see 75 to 80 new people each week and most of them would come back every two weeks and have four or five lessons in a series. Some from Leongatha and that area have come back for lessons since 1960.

I have also taught most of the Metropolitan members at one time or another, and some I have taught since they were young juniors. I have taught some members all their golfing lives which, in some cases, is now adding up to over 63 years. Many of my long-time Metro pupils have had hundreds of free and incidental lessons with me, too.

I had a large following of keen golfers from far and wide who would come back for years, and many still come back today, or will just ring me and I can fix their problem over the phone. As they have grown older, many need their swings and clubs adapted to keep playing, which I am always happy to do. I have loved teaching in the city and the country and on TV. I think I'd even be happy to teach golf underwater, if it ever came to that.

'I had about 15 paid lessons at the most, but because we have been away with Brian so often, I would have had 150 to 200 additional lessons, no exaggeration. Often when I am on the driving range hitting a bucket of balls, Brian would give me a lesson and I would go home to Helen and say "I have been Twited", which means he sends me to the wilderness for about a week while I try to apply it, and then once I've done that, I'm on to the next stage.'

Dr Bill Kimber, Metro member

Lessons to the many notables

The Governors

Sir Dallas Brooks was a very keen golfer and he became one of my regulars. As Governor of Victoria, he became an honorary member. All the Victorian governors, and earlier Australian governors general who lived in Melbourne, were invited to Metropolitan in those days.

I played with him once every four or five weeks. This started not long after I arrived at Metropolitan. One afternoon, the manager, Mr Kissling, came up to say the Governor was coming out to play and he wanted a game with me, so I had to cancel all my lessons. Everyone understood, because the Governor was No. 1.

Sir Dallas – it was always 'Sir Dallas' if we were with other people, or just 'Sir' when we were playing together – was on a four handicapper.

His handicap never moved, so he didn't really need any help; he just wanted someone to play with. He was a wonderful putter, far better than I was. He said to me: 'You know, Brian, if you had my putting, we'd beat the world.'

Sir Dallas played at several clubs and regularly organised team events at them where he would always lead the Governor's team. In 1955, he became the patron of Metropolitan's mixed foursomes' championship, named after him, and it remains a major event, played every year at Metropolitan.

He played with Joan Fisher, one of Australia's greatest amateur champions, and a member of Metropolitan among other clubs, and they got to the semi-finals twice, I think, but never won it.

Played over a week, it's a very difficult tournament to win. I've been in the semi-finals three or four times with Shirley Nagle, but we've never been successful. Sir Dallas also had a house on the second hole down at Little Frankston, the Frankston course. He was a real enthusiast.

I also played with Sir Brian Murray, who was Governor of Victoria from 1982 to 1985. He had about half a dozen lessons before a big event at Royal Melbourne. He was off 24, a bad 24, and hardly ever played.

One day he came over for a lesson and said: 'Brian, I'm very nervous. I'm playing Royal Melbourne today in front of all these people because it's Governor's Day. What if I hit a bad shot?' I said: 'Well, it's like this. If you hit a good shot, they'll applaud you. If you hit a bad shot, they'll be silent, and then all you've got to say is: 'Brian Twite told me this is a very difficult golf course', and they'll all laugh.'

That's exactly what happened. He hit it about 10 feet on the first tee, and he just said: 'Brian Twite told me this is a hard golf course.' He went off down the fairway and they all clapped him.

Then Sir Brian bought one of those swing machines we used to sell where you stand inside and swing within the arc. He had it at Government House so he could practise at work, but he stayed on 24. He didn't play much and didn't get any lower, but I did get him to hit the ball very well. I think he played with me only twice at Metro and he played every year with the Governor and amateur team at the Governor's Day, in Barwon Heads. He didn't play it well.

I did play a lot with Sir Henry Winneke in the 1960s. He started off on a 15 handicap and got down to about 12, so he was good. He played nearly every week on a Sunday with his secretary, Bill Shelton. Sir Henry had so much humour. He would always say: 'Great shot, but wrong direction.' He was wonderful to play with. You wouldn't think he was the Governor; he just acted like one of the members, and everyone called him 'Henry'. He was the first Winneke to join Metropolitan, followed in time by his sons, Michael and Jack. They are a wonderful family. Over the years, I was often invited to garden parties at Government House which I enjoyed immensely.

I also gave lessons to Peter Reith, a former Cabinet Minister, down at the driving range in later years. He was quite a good player. He knew where he was going. He was 6 foot 2 inches and a powerful man.

Googie Withers had quite a few lessons with me at Metro after she arrived from England to live in Australia in the late 1950s. She was a charming girl who played off an 18 handicap. She had good rhythm but, being a dancer, had the fault of swaying back and forth. She had a great sense of humour, too. One of the older members said to me: 'How can you teach that kid?' I said: 'Why?' He replied: 'Well, because she wears the lowest tops I've ever seen.'

Googie Withers from the film Loves of Joanna Godden, 1947

Googie gave me her dog when she was going to London for a new play and couldn't take it with her. I have a photo with her dog and my original MacGregor clubs and the golf bag which I brought with me to Australia. The shot was taken on the practice fairway outside the shop. There was a group of nine pine trees between the practice fairway and the first fairway where our putting green is now. They were all taken down when the fairway was widened.

On the practice fairway with Googie Wither's dog, circa 1957

Sadly, one Sunday when I was going off to play in an event at Victoria Golf Club, we accidentally ran over and killed Googie's dog. My driver, who was taking me to Victoria, didn't see the dog because, he was sandy-coloured, being a Corgi, and was lying on the sandy path near my driveway.

I had rounds of 71, 73, 74 in the

tournament and was already six over after four holes in the final day round when General Robertson, from Metro, took me aside and blew hell out of me. 'You just think that you can play like that because you've killed a dog? That's nothing, now put it out of your mind. Act like a professional, be a professional, and try like a professional, otherwise you can carry your own clubs.'

I played the next 14 holes in four under the card for a 74. Afterwards, the General, who always called me 'Twite', came over and said: 'Brian, I'm very proud of you. You've played exactly the way I wanted you to play. I knew exactly what I could do to get you out of your mood. That's why I'm a general.' It had worked — forget the past, Twitey, just think in the present, and that's the most valuable lesson I've learned.

Teaching in the city

This program started the year after I came to Melbourne. In those days, the biggest sports stores used to host golf lessons for their customers. I was invited to give clinics in the city for a while, but it didn't last for long. The PGA decided that giving golf lessons in stores was against the regulations and we would be suspended if we continued, so we stopped it.

Brian Twite advertisement, Argus, 2 August 1956

113

Teaching in the country

The Victorian Golf Foundation and the Victorian Ladies' Golf Union

The Victorian Golf Association (now Golf Victoria) was originally called the Victorian Golf Foundation, and Bill Edgar was in charge. In the 1930s, Bill was called Australia's Bobby Jones. He won three Victorian and two South Australian amateur titles between 1927 and 1951. He was a legend in amateur golf. In the 1970s and 1980s, Bill, Jock Williams and I used to tour around the country encouraging youngsters to play golf at local clubs that didn't have a club professional. We went every Friday rotating between Bairnsdale, Korumburra, Leongatha, Yallourn and Castlemaine golf clubs. After we'd played 18 holes, usually an exhibition match, we would give them lessons and then have a film night in their clubhouse.

There were also golf training camps for junior boys and girls. The boys' camp was at Geelong, and the girls' camp, which was started in the mid-1960s by Miss Burtta Cheney and the VLGU (Victorian Ladies' Golf Union), was at Anglesea.

Miss Cheney had a long career in amateur golf and won an Australian Championship, represented Australia numerous times and even visited Sunningdale in the late 1950s where she reported back that they were missing me. Miss Cheney was very proper, but not without a sense of humour. While we always agreed on the golf fundamentals and how to teach them, she did ask me to change 'thumbs up to the sky' to 'thumbs pointing to the sky' on the backswing. She thought 'thumbs up' was an unsuitable expression for girls. A group of club professionals and leading women amateurs would go to Anglesea to teach for that week in December every year. I loved doing that.

Leongatha

For years I rotated between teaching at Castlemaine or Geelong and Leongatha on Fridays. In hindsight, I was crazy to do that. I've been lucky to be blessed with enormous stamina, maybe because I was on the farm for a long time. In the summer, during the harvest, you'd work morning from 4.00 am until 11.00 pm and thought nothing of it. So working seven days a week as a pro was easy for me.

Kit Boag with Brian, Leongatha Golf Club, 1987

I first went to Leongatha as part of a Golf Foundation event held there to teach all the juniors in the area. My regular trips began in May 1977 when I was invited by Olive Harris, the VLGU delegate for South Gippsland, to give a clinic for junior girls in the area.

Coral Gray, Brian Twite, Val Brydon and Dot Stubbs of the winning Leongatha team in 2009

As there were so few juniors, I agreed to teach the ladies, too, and then opened the clinics to everyone. They really liked it and by lunchtime they'd asked me to come down once a month. I agreed, and I used to

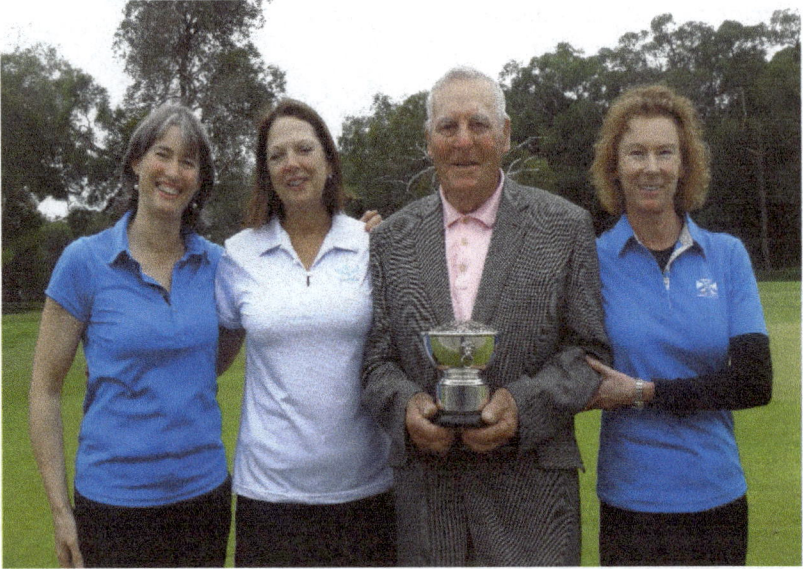

Jay Bethell, Julie Kirk, Brian Twite and Lisa Parkinson, the winning Metropolitan team in 2014

'Brian was an excellent teacher who was extremely generous with his time and advice. He taught at least five club champions, men and women, in their formative golfing years. His teaching methods were widely appreciated. He didn't try to radically change your swing. He had the ability to see what you were doing and improve it without a lot of pain. He was always very encouraging, too. One day, he was giving my daughter a putting lesson and had lent her a putter to help her stop three-putting. He said: "If you can get down in two putts, I will let you have the putter." She did, and he gave her the putter. It was a good one, too.'

Jon Smith, club historian, Leongatha GC

give 20-minute lessons from 8.30 am to 5.00 pm. and People would put their names for lessons on a list in the clubhouse. A dear girl, Kit Boag, controlled the clinics. Kitty would be on that fairway all day. She'd pick up every ball and would let everyone know: 'Your lesson is for 20 minutes. If you're two minutes late, you get 18 minutes,' and they all came and they had 20-minute lessons.

I used to leave at 6.00 am and get home at 7.00 pm. I did that until 1986 when Leongatha finally put on their own professional. As a parting gift, I donated a silver rose bowl as a perpetual trophy for a competition of their choice and the club introduced the Brian Twite Annual Bowl. This has become a popular and prestigious event in Leongatha and South Gippsland.

Leongatha is a very friendly club and I've got good relationships there. People still ring me for follow-up phone

'It was a privilege to work with Brian Twite, a wonderful teacher for young and old. He came to Leongatha in May 1977. He did a clinic for South Gippsland juniors in the afternoon. I filled in the morning with ladies and, as each one came in, I asked if they would come back again. By lunchtime, we asked the question of Brian and he agreed – once a month on a Friday. I always had a full day booked. Many club champions followed – Val Brighton, Rea Stewart, Robyn Dennis, Beth Stubbs, Russell Dunes, Darren Green among them. I feel very privileged that Brian came back and played on my golf day each year.

What helped me most was him saying: "Stand, grip correctly, and for an exercise, throw the club forward and back, shoulder high, then swing through to the sky and take your right leg with you." I learnt so much from Brian and by working with him and asking him questions, I was able to help so many others.'

Kit Boag, Leongatha GC

lessons. I still go down to Leongatha each year to play in the Kit Boag Mixed Canadian Foursomes and to present the Brian Twite Trophy. I have been delighted to present it many times to the local Leongatha team and to our Metro girls Jay Bethell, Lisa Parkinson and Julie Kirk, who won it recently for the second time.

Photographic memory – that's what teaching is all about

Gary Player taught me this 50 years ago – you need a really good photographic memory because that's what teaching is all about.

A gentleman from Western Australia comes over every year for two weeks and has four lessons from me. One year he said to me: 'I'm going home next week. What can I tell my friend Vern?'

I'd given Vern a lesson some time before. 'Tell Vern two things,' I replied, then detailed the two things.

'How can you remember that?' he asked.

'I know everyone's swing,' I said. 'I look at people and my mind goes back to their swing.'

It's a natural thing that you learn as a teacher. The sheer volume of people I've taught helps. I've probably given 150,000 to 200,000 lessons. As most would have more than one lesson, I have probably taught around 50,000 people.

> 'I think Brian has eyes in the back of his head. If you say to Brian that your shots are doing this, that or the other, he'll reply: "I saw you on the 16th approaching the green and you were doing this, that or the other." That is his genius. He sees everybody's swing and knows what's wrong within seconds, almost as they set up to the ball, and then he adjusts your swing, and will keep adjusting it until you get it.
>
> Helen Kimber, friend and Metro member

Introducing the first camera

Years ago, a normal golf lesson would cost 17/6, but I used to charge 30 shillings, not because the lessons were longer – they weren't – but I had a special attraction: a new camera, which I bought especially to photograph my pupils. The camera took eight pictures at intervals of one sixth of a second. Then seconds after the pictures had been taken, the camera produced the eight photos.

The results were startling in some cases. I had one player who I had been trying to convince for six weeks that he was keeping his left leg stiff during his swing. The player thought he was bending his leg, but it was not until he saw the film that he realised it was as stiff as a poker. The next time he bent his knee correctly.

'Before I joined Metro in 1977, I used to sneak on to the course with my great friend, Mike Clayton. Brian knew we were there.

Mike and I used one of the first reel-to-reel video tape recorders invented and which I borrowed from the sports science department at Rusden. Prior to that the camera''' was a great fascination and we used to borrow Brian's when he wasn't around or wasn't using it. I don't think we ever paid a cent for the film, though. We were cheapskate students at the time and Brian was a very generous person.

He was so generous with his time and equipment. I remember we were playing one evening back in 1976 and Brian came out of the pro shop to proudly show us a new Wilson 1200 driver that he had fitted with a graphite shaft, something very new at the time. Mike and I were suitably impressed and wanted to give it a crack straight away. My first drive with this club went in the cross-bunkers on the first. I'd never been in them before and I haven't been in them since. On the fifth, I repeated the dose into the cross-bunkers not far short of the green. I have witnesses. Needless to say I was sold, and that driver went into my bag immediately and I don't think Brian ever saw it again.'

Clyde Boyer, player and Metro member

CAMERA IS A FAULT FINDER

GOLF NOTES .... by KEN KNOX

A normal golf lesson costs 17/6, Metropolitan professional Brian te is charging 30/- for some of lessons.

The lessons are no longer than al, but they have a special attrac-

Brian recently bought a new camera to photograph his pupils.

The camera takes eight pictures at intervals of 1/6th of a second.

Then seconds after the pictures have been taken the camera produces the eight photos.

The results have been startling in some cases.

In one case Brian had been trying to convince a player for six weeks that he was keeping his left leg stiff during his swing.

The player thought he was bending his leg, but it was not until he saw the photos that he accepted Brian as right.

The next time he bent his knee correctly.

Golf pro on HSV

Brian Twite (Metropolitan) is the pro featured on Colin Long's Golf Clinic on HSV7's World Of Sport tomorrow.

BRIAN TWITE using his camera during lessons with assistant Mel McLennan.

Photos of junior member Gillian Ednie taken with the new camera, circa 1973

Teaching golf on TV

World of Sport

I was also fortunate to be one of the pros regularly featured on Colin Long's golf segment on Channel Seven's *World of Sport*. Sadie Ann and I have fond memories of that program and I can remember working with Jack Dyer, Doug Elliott, who owned the show, Ron Casey and Lou Richards.

The studio was in South Melbourne and I can recall exactly the layout, the stage and the casual, haphazard atmosphere. One day, Sadie Ann and I were called up to do the advertisement for Patra orange juice and Hutton's ham. It went something like: 'Everybody loves Patra orange juice, even Twite's daughter likes Patra orange juice.' It was very impromptu, and Sadie Ann and I used to love the show with all its fun and drama.

Lou Richards really didn't like me. Colin Long used to ask: 'Brian, bring in a bucket of sand,' so I brought a big bucket of sand, and they had an eight-foot net in a bunker and I'd play shots over the net. Lou would then come over and give me a six-foot brush.

'You can't come and mess up my show, sweep up the bloody stuff.' I'd take the brush and I'd sweep it up.

One day, I was cleaning my teeth and I thought: 'I'll fix that little devil,' so put a toothbrush in my pocket. The next time I played the bunker shots over the net.

Lou said: 'You can't come in here, Twite, and make that mess. Here's the brush.'

'I've brought my own brush,' I said, and took out my toothbrush. He was stunned. He couldn't speak for 20 seconds and everybody was roaring their heads off. Later he complained: 'You set me up.'

They got so many phone calls to say how brilliant the segment was. Lou was not happy.

I did the golf segment on *World of Sport* for eight or nine years and it was a good show. I had a segment every five or six weeks on rotation with several other pros, such as Tony Greenhill, Howard Hutchinson, Brian Huxtable and Geoff Flanagan.

Colin would invite people, regardless of whether they were a trainee professional or a visiting superstar. First he would interview the guest and then get them to hit a few balls into a net set up in the studio to allow their swings to be analysed on a new-fangled slow-motion camera. Some pros were a little volatile and balls would be flying everywhere, but Colin was unflappable.

One time we filmed the segment at Metro and I said to Colin: 'Look, people don't want to see me playing the first hole with a drive, an iron and two putts. Why don't I hit my ball into the fairway bunker, then put it in the next bunker on the right of the green, get it out to 20 feet and knock it in for four?'

He agreed. I played dozens of shots and he recorded them on the course and did the running commentary. When I was in the greenside bunker, Colin said: 'Brian's got a struggle now to get a four.'

I walked in and played the bunker shot a long way from the hole. 'He's got a hell of a job to put this putt in,' Colin declared, and after five putts, it went in. People enjoyed it because it was something they wanted to see. They didn't want to see good shots all the time. So we did that quite often. I would tell them how to play a shot and show them how I played that shot. For example, in the bunker, I'd say: 'Stand up tall, keep your right shoulder high, don't let your right shoulder down otherwise you will hit the club too deeply into the sand.'

That section would be recorded, we would replay it in the studio, and I'd speak to it and give the lesson. One day, Colin said: 'What would a 30-handicapper do on the first tee?' and I said: 'They'd probably top it.'

'Would you mind topping it?' So Colin then introduced me. 'Here is one of the best professionals in Australia, a wonderful golfer, and he is now hitting off the first tee,' and it went about 15 feet.

The Happy Hammond Tarax Show

When Tony Charlton, a GTV 9 sports commentator, wanted to encourage children to play golf, he asked me to help. As part of the Happy Hammond Show, we had 100 children at the Channel 9 studios in Bendigo Street coming in three times a week for golf coaching.

With the help of Tony and Ranald Macdonald, we took in three carloads of 10- and 11-year-old kids from the local area (two of whom became low markers and members of Huntingdale), and a group of young Metro caddies, among them John Smith. One day, John was standing in a line with the other kids, all swinging clubs, when he hit one in the jaw with his five-iron, live on television.

After a month, a staggering 1000 children turned up at East Malvern driving range for a children's golf clinic which was opened by the Governor, Sir Dallas Brooks. Because it rained, the number dropped to about 400, which was still a massive number to manage. We had them in lines and taught them the basic swing in three positions – arms out, break wrists and swing club back to shoulder height. It was a great success, but sadly it was a one-off promotion.

Teaching the Associates at Metro

I always gave special attention to the lady and junior members as they were often overlooked in the club and were always so appreciative of the time I spent with them. As a form of encouragement, I donated a perpetual trophy in 1960 for the best two out of three Stableford rounds played on a Tuesday in July, August and September every year, which is still played for today.

Over the years, there were some very fine golfers and great characters among the 'Associates', as they were called before 1984 when equal opportunity legislation was introduced and women became 'members'. Great names of the 1960s and 1970s come to mind, like Joan Dixon, who was a superb golfer and a flamboyant personality. Any time you saw Joan playing from the trees, you just knew her next shot would be on the green and she'd win the hole.

Nell Smithett was a scratch golfer and the complete opposite. She was an excellent golfer who came over from Huntingdale to be our handicapper.

Then there were the great characters like Marie Carlyon, who was always immaculately dressed, and, regardless of the weather, her hair never moved. She was inspirational and a magnificent pennant captain. She won two pennants for us, including a First Division flag in 1965, and the girls said they won for Marie, rather than the club.

Others notable for their graciousness and longevity were Mary Syme and Jacqui Harris. Both served in many roles, including president. Betty McLaughlin was our biggest character, always funny and famous for her much-loved impersonations of the Queen, which came out at all important club occasions.

Winning First Division Pennant team 1965, with Marie Carlyon second on the left and Joan Fisher, third from the right, 1965

Jocelyn Fitzhardinge was another character. From Canberra, she was a tall, bronzed, physical education teacher and a gifted golfer, but often so intense she would be overwhelmed if she wasn't playing well.

I taught everyone in both pennant teams. Apart from helping them with their swings and technical shots like up and downhill and rough lies, as we didn't have many of those at Metro, I also worked on their confidence. As I taught half the pennant players in other clubs, too, I knew their abilities, how they were going to play and how they thought.

As the order of the teams didn't change much in those days, I could give our players odds on how they might fare against their most likely opposite numbers in each team. Mostly, I could give them positive odds, for example: 'You will beat so and so four out of every six matches.' I supported this with a talk about their opponent's relative strengths and weaknesses. Whatever the odds, and especially if they were not so good, I would still say: 'You can win on the day, so be ready to play your best golf. You can do it.' I wanted to give them as much confidence and belief in themselves as I could, which can often be the most important thing in a match. I also enjoyed receiving all the post-match results and stories, whether their strategies had worked well or not, and what they could do next time.

I also had to manage any personal conflicts on occasions, most famously with two of Metro's finest older golfers. Joan Fisher was a multiple Australian and Victorian champion, international team player, club champion and more. Bettine Burgess was also a distinguished amateur player with several state titles and club championships to her name. Bettine and Joan could not abide each other. If they were ever drawn together, I had to work it out. Bettine would simply stay in the locker room until I put someone else with

Joan. When they had to play matches against each other, they just didn't speak, but Joan was like that in matches whoever she played.

Among the great players I taught from outside the club was Dawn Denhert (later McDonald). She was a gifted amateur from Barwon Heads and she is still playing today. Another was Margie Masters, from Woodlands. She won five Victorian championships and national championships in four countries (Australia, New Zealand, Canada and South Africa) before becoming one of Australia's first female golf professionals in 1965. Later I also gave a few lessons to Jane Crafter, who was a very successful amateur golfer from South Australia before joining the LPGA tour in 1981 and becoming a golf commentator, as she remains today.

Teaching the children and the juniors

I have always loved teaching the children and grandchildren of members. On children's day, we would line them up and get them hitting balls, having a few chips and putts, and then inside for party food – a great combination.

During the 1960s and 1970s, I also gave lessons to school children and teenagers in school programs where I could. I taught at Murrumbeena High School, Oakleigh Technical School, Sacre Coeur Girls' School, and

'As a child, I really enjoyed having a lesson with Brian, and probably enjoyed the mudcake afterwards even more. Brian was always so welcoming. My brother, David, and I felt like treasured little units. We learnt to play golf and this is where my love of putting began. While Brian and Dad were talking, I would keep putting, which I thought had to be the easiest part of the game because the ball was closest to the hole.'

Chris Faram, Metro member

'My mother took me to Brian's children's clinics when I was about eight. In the 1970s, Brian taught me to swing, and 20 years later he also taught my children at children's days and anytime he saw us. Brian would interrupt whatever he was doing to give us his time and encouragement. He would always compliment the kids and tell my daughter, Isabel, what a beautiful name she had.'

Pam Kelton, Metro member

'I first met Brian in 1964, when I was just 19. I had come down from Queensland to play in an intervarsity tournament at Metropolitan. At that time, Metropolitan was really nice to juniors. Brian was teaching some of the Monash students, one of which was my future husband, Geoff (Leeton), and Metro gave us the course for nothing – that kindness and generosity was pretty amazing. And they gave us dinner for $2. I had curried scallops. Before our first game, the Melbourne girls came up and said, "Oh, the pro here will give everybody a quick lesson, if we all line up." So that's how I met Brian Twite. There were eight teams of six girls, nearly fifty girls, and he got to every single one of us before we teed off and gave everyone a free lesson.'

Dr Kay Leeton, friend and Metro member

Melbourne High. Golf was featured as part of their sporting program which was a great thing when it was offered.

When Monash University opened in Clayton, I held clinics for students which Professor Bryan Hudson (Metropolitan member and later president) helped organise. Initially, I took 400 balls and 50 clubs and ran a clinic on one of the campus ovals. The students were also invited to play here on Wednesdays at midday. This relationship dramatically broke down, however, when a group of four students went from bunker to bunker on the sixth green, oblivious to the fact that they were holding up Dr Crapp, Pat Ramsden, Bill Priestley and

Brian Faram, who watched with mounting anger behind them. The students continued to have individual free lessons with me and play on the course, but not in groups.

I also gave lessons to the university students that played at Metropolitan as part of their intervarsity competitions.

'I am always so grateful to Brian. I had lessons with him when I was at Amstel. He coached me and got me into Metropolitan, and really looked after me. My parents were far away in Inverloch and he was like a father-figure coach to me when I really needed that support.'

Debbie Baulch, Metro member

I have always taken a special interest in juniors and their development as golfers, and I have also enjoyed getting to know them as adults. I remember the young Garton twins, Anne and Debbie, and how Debbie (now Baulch) became a fine golfer with a lifelong passion for golf.

The best junior I taught

Rarely would I find a super talented junior, and Ann Joyce (now Johnston) was the finest I ever taught. Her mother had heard I was pretty good at teaching youngsters, so she brought Ann down from Seymour to see me for lessons in 1974 when Ann was about thirteen or fourteen.

Ann continued coming over the years, and when I heard she was thinking of leaving home and moving to Melbourne, I told her mother: 'If you like, Ann can come and stay with us for 12 months. I've got two daughters and a boy at home, and a spare room.'

Ann was the same age as my Susie and they became great friends. She stayed with us for 12 months and played golf and got down from an eight-handicap to scratch. She was very tall and strong because she had worked on a farm, and she was a natural swinger. I got her into Metro as a junior where she joined Debbie Garton and Lee Carrington, who later became a professional and taught in Singapore.

Ann could have become a professional. There was an offer from an American professional who thought she was brilliant when she was only 17 or 18. However, her mother wasn't keen, and neither was Ann – she wasn't a girl who wanted to travel overseas on her own and knew she was happy to stay in Australia.

Instead, she worked part-time and played amateur golf. She was in the state junior and then senior teams, won the Victorian Championship in 1993, and helped Metro win a couple of Division 2 pennant flags in the 1980s.

Ann Johnston winning the Victorian Women's Amateur Championship in 1993

On a different front, she had many suitors, most of whom were unsuitable, and I had to bat them off, until one of our best greenskeepers, Tony Johnston, said to me: 'I'm going to marry that girl.' I said to Tony: 'Well, if you want to get a hold of Ann, you've just got to send her roses every week', and he did. At first, Ann wasn't very interested, but eventually she was, and they later married and now have three lovely children.

Ladies pennant team, from left: Lee Carrington, Ann Johnston, Kay Leeton, Jeanne McMullin, Debbie Baulch, Gillian Ednie, Jenny Fawcett, 1987

The current junior scholarship program

While I had always encouraged and supported juniors to play and keep playing, it was recently recognised that Metro was not getting enough juniors coming through the regular membership. Manager Allan Shoreland, to his credit, looked at other clubs here and overseas and found a junior scholarship program we could copy.

It was introduced in 2008 and it has been a marvellous success. We developed a training program and gave the juniors mentors over their 12 months with us. I ran the training clinic on the first Sunday of the month and gave them individual lessons as well.

Some were already fantastic golfers, such as Todd Sinnott and Su Hyan Oh, both of whom have become outstanding professionals. We have helped Blake Collier and Grace Daniel and many others develop to a standard where they have been chosen in state and national teams, while the program has also added needed strength and depth to our pennant teams. Both the men's and women's teams have since won Division 1 flags. The women won back to back pennants in 2013 and 14 breaking a long drought back to 1965 when Joan Fisher and Marie Carlyon were in the winning team, and the men have won twice in the last three years in 2016 and 2018. Over the years, some 130 kids have come through the program, many of whom stayed to become junior and young club members.

– CHAPTER 11 –

My fundamentals of golf

From my earliest years in King's Lynn, I had been taught the fundamentals of golf and the golf swing by many wonderful teachers and players. For me, they all said the same things, and these are the things that have always worked for me. They have become my fundamentals of golf and I still teach them to this day.

Building on the natural swing

Everybody has a natural talent somewhere, and I was always taught to use that natural talent. Harold Atkinson at Abbeydale was the first to teach me to watch the person to see what his or her natural talent was, and then emphasise to them that it's the clubhead that's going to hit the ball, not the swing. Arthur Lees at Sunningdale also taught me to look at people to identify how that fellow's doing this or this girl is doing that, and work on that. He said we must never try to change the natural ability of the swing or to manufacture the swing. If somebody swings the club naturally, build around it. And that's what I've always done, and it has always been successful.

The golf swing is an easy thing if you don't make it complicated. We make it complicated when we try and copy other people. Golf professionals make it complicated when they try to copy someone like Adam Scott, for example.

For example, convincing some people to use the clubhead, and not their swing, to hit the ball is one of the hardest things to teach. Players have to know in their own mind where the clubhead is to hit the ball with their natural hit, their natural 'knowing'. I have had to find different ways to make this point. For example, if it was a man who could use a hammer I would say: 'Hit it like you hit a nail', because he instinctively knows where the hammer head is to knock in the nail. And if it was a teacher, I would say: 'Who is the naughtiest boy in your class? Now hit that naughty boy on the bottom as hard as you can.' Of course, I can't say this nowadays.

'It was extraordinary the way Brian would stand on one leg, swing his club around his back and do all this swivelling business, then say: "It doesn't matter what happens at any part of the swing, it's what happens when the club hits the ball." Every lesson he'd do the same thing - stand on one leg and swivel around like Jim Furyk on steroids, and then hit this amazing shot every time. It stuck in my mind. He was a remarkable teacher. He always found a way to demonstrate his point and it would absolutely stick in my mind.'

Caroline Nicholson,
Metro member

Adapting the fundamentals to the player, not the player to the fundamentals

The fundamentals of golf, or the basics of the golf swing, are the same the world over, but when you're teaching you must remember that everybody is different. It doesn't matter where you are, you must adapt the fundamentals to the ability of the person, not the person to the fundamentals. You simply can't teach one method to everyone because you can't apply those fundamentals in the same way to the tall fellow, the heavy fellow, the small fellow, or the big fellow. They can't swing the club the same way.

I have seen so many ordinary and great players try to replace their natural swing with a manufactured swing and they have always been disappointed. Clyde Boyer is a great example. He was brilliant and could even hit the 16th green with his driver across the dogleg. He was having great scores and was captain of the Victorian team. However, against my advice, he wanted to change his hands at the top of his swing. He worked on the practice fairway for six months with a video recorder until he got into the perfect position, but it didn't work. He hasn't played at that level since. Clyde said to me when he was here recently: 'Twite, if only I had listened to you, but I didn't have enough sense. I wanted to be better and searched relentlessly for a better swing.'

We always feel we want to be better than we are, and we're always looking for the secret. You've got to have enough

'As teacher, Brian has had a profound impact my golf and on me personally. Over the years, he has given me hundreds of lessons helping me with little incremental things. Through his unusual teaching method, I came down from 15 to 5 at Kew Golf Club before I joined Metro a few years ago. He doesn't try to rebuild swings, he just works with you and gives you one or two things to think about at each time, and apparently, that's method is coming back. I heard Greg Norman being interviewed the other day and one of the commentators said, "There's a lot of different swings around at the moment, Greg." To which Greg went on to say, "People are working with people's natural swings much more these days rather than trying to teach the one swing to everybody." That's been Brian's mantra.'

Stephen Enright, stepson and Metro member

common sense to go through your scores, and if you're scoring 73s but you want to score 71s, it may be as simple as making a putt or two. It's not the long game but the short game from 50 metres that's going to get you from a one handicap to plus three.

Rory McIlroy was killing himself for 18 months because he changed his swing. He's getting back now. He's going back to the way he normally was. You look at Tiger Woods. Tiger's shoulders were nice and slim, and they moved beautifully. Then he goes to the gym and they became four feet wide. His arms cannot cope with his shoulders. They think if they get buffed up they hit the ball harder. They might do that, but they lose the feeling of the clubhead. Tiger Woods has made a comeback. Now he's slimmer, he's much thinner, and I think he will play quite well.

Over the years, a lot of these players, and some of our youngsters at Metro, changed their natural swings. They might not agree, but I'm sure they would have been better off if they had trusted and kept their natural swings, rather than trying to manufacture something else.

The best example, of course, is Ian Baker-Finch. How can you hit a ball out of bounds on the Old Course at St Andrew's? You have to be 250 yards left of the fairway. After having a brilliant 64 and going on to win the British Open at Royal Birkdale, the poor man tried to change his swing, and he never recovered it.

Belief and confidence – managing the inner game

After building on a player's natural swing and adapting the fundamentals to their swing, the next most important thing, and my favourite thing as a teacher, is to get people to believe in themselves. This is the hardest thing to do.

Belief and confidence go together. You must be confident in what you're doing and don't hesitate. If you hesitate, you are lost. When you're swinging well, your mind is free, and your muscles and mind are working together. But once you have doubt in your mind, your mind starts fighting your muscles. They must work together.

Belief starts from the very beginning – from your first thoughts about a shot. Recently I had a fellow having persistent bunker trouble and he said: 'Every time I go into a bunker, Brian, I know I'm not going to get it out. What do I do?'

'Well,' I said, 'I was in the left-hand bunker on the 7th a few weeks ago. I walked in and put it two feet from the hole. The fellow I was playing with said: "You didn't take any time, Brian." I said: "Yes I did. I've taken 10 minutes to play that shot. As soon as I left that tee, I knew how I was going to play that shot. As I walked down the fairway, I knew exactly that the pin was 20 feet away and I knew exactly the speed I had to hit the ball, and I just walked in and played it as I had planned."'

Gary Player told me this 50 years ago. He also taught me about positive self-talk, or 'affirmations' as they are called today. I remember the first time Gary came to play in the Australian Ampol Tournament at Yarra Yarra in 1956. He gave a clinic on the practice fairway in which he said to believe in yourself – you've got to talk to yourself. I asked him if he talked to himself. 'Yes, I talk to myself whether I play nine holes, 18 holes, or tournament golf. I always talk to myself and say things like: "I am a great putter, I'm a great golfer and I believe in myself."'

I watched him in the practice round (you could walk alongside the players in those days) and I could hear him saying 'I'm a good putter, I'm a good putter, I'm a good putter' all the way to the green.

He emphasised more than anyone that you had to believe in yourself. He didn't have to worry about his golf swing. He knew he was going to put it on the green, and he did. The next year he won the Australian Open at Kooyonga, the first of his seven Open victories during the 1960s and '70s. He also won the Wills Masters in 1968.

I teach people to start preparing for the next shot as soon as possible. When you're walking down to your next shot you're thinking: 'How do I want to play this shot?' When you get to the ball, you only have to adapt yourself to the lie because you've already made yourself believe that you're going to play the shot you want.

Belief always comes first. You can't change your method or your swing without changing your thinking and believing in that change first. The same applies to visualising your shots – you have to believe it before you can see it. If you don't believe, you won't see it.

'Brian first started teaching me when I played interclub. He said I just need to change your swing a little bit, and through the season he very gently changed my swing and it improved so much he has taught me ever since. He understands my swing and everything about it so well that he can even diagnose me over the phone.

The most important thing he has taught me is to accept your shot even though it's far from what was planned. He will still say, "That's magnificent!", he uses that word a lot. He has also taught me to say "thank you" when someone gives you a compliment for a shot, no matter what you think about it. On the mental game he has taught me not to panic when I get into trouble and to be confident with my putts. He has got me to say, "I am a good putter, I am a really good putter, I can put this, I know I am a really good putter", and it works.

Brian is more than just a professional, he is the person who is interested in your golf, he will ask how you are going, and if you have any issues. He is also great to have a friendly round with. We have lots of fun and laughs together, the golf is serious, but we do laugh a lot too. He is incredibly supportive, and I feel so fortunate to have such a wonderful relationship with him. I refer to him as the Master and myself as his apprentice. It is a very special relationship; its more than a coach or mentor, he really cares and is always so patient. Even when I say, "Sorry Brian I know I have come to you before with this problem, but I just can't remember the solution," and he'll say, "Now Jay, let's go back to your fundamentals". Of course, I will remember then.

As the old saying goes, "He has taught me everything I know, but not everything he knows", so, happily, I still have a few more lessons to go.'

Jay Bethell, Metro member

As Arnold Palmer has said, 'Golf is a game of inches. The most important are the six inches between your ears', and he was absolutely right. If you look at the amateur player, and even the professionals, you can see them on the tee or playing their shots and thinking: 'What am I going to do with it? How am I going to do it?' They're lost before they start. Some people can manage it, but the majority of amateur golfers can't manage that level of uncertainty or doubt. Their concentration is so scattered, it's not on one point. When on the golf course, you must focus on one point or have one thought only in your mind when you are hitting the ball.

The most important 'one thought' I teach is to keep your head still and, even more importantly, to keep your eyes on the back of the ball and to keep those eyes still. If your eyes move, your head moves. You can move your head like Freddy Couples does, but his eyes stay still on the ball.

If you can keep your eyes still all the time, you can have a different 'one thought', such as my favourite which is to accelerate through the ball. Don't think about your swing technicals, such as turn away here or there, or the top part of my body sways, and the club must not get out of line, that's for the practice fairway and practice swing. Instead, just keep your eyes still on the ball, trust yourself and hit the ball with your natural hit, and that's it.

Playing in the zone

The ultimate state of belief and confidence which allows you to play your best golf is called 'the zone'. It's a wonderful state of mind which happens when you are totally present in the moment, your mind is clear and focused on one thought at a time only, your swing is natural and effortless, and everything goes right. It can be elusive, but there are ways to get there and stay there.

First, you must feel that you really know the course. This is easy when you have played your home course a thousand times. It's easy then to make a plan and mentally rehearse where you are going to stand on each tee, and where you will hit to on every hole and so on.

Next, you decide on how you are going to play the course. You have to figure out if you can hit the ball straight or will you have to manoeuvre it by fading or drawing the ball into the greens. Once you are on the course, you've got to visualise your shots in the air and where you want them to land and to finish. Then, when you are hitting the ball, you can think of only one thing — one thought that is going to make your swing work.

The actual swing thought can vary, but once chosen, it must be the same swing thought all the way around the golf course, not a rotation of half a dozen different points.

For me, I choose to be conscious of accelerating the clubhead through the ball. I think the same thought for everything, whether it's driving, chipping, putting or bunkers. If you slow down on the way through, as so many people do, you get a lazy swing, you move forward, and your hands are late, and the ball is off to the right. You still have to keep your eyes on the ball (which should be a habit), but if you don't accelerate the club at the bottom of the swing, you are not going to hit the ball correctly.

If you do have a wobble, a three-putt or anything that disrupts your concentration, the quickest way to get back into the zone is simply to breathe out before you hit the ball. Most people miss short puts because they get too tense and tight in their chest, which affects everything else and they stop breathing. Jack Nicklaus always breathes out before he hits the ball, so he can swing freely with all his natural ability. That's one of the best secrets of the whole game.

Love of the game

I never tire of helping people to improve their golf and their enjoyment of the game. It's just as rewarding for me now as it always has been. I love hearing about their successes, such as reducing their handicap, winning a match or even a club championship.

I am also there for them when they need some kind words and wisdom to overcome their disappointments. I love being part of the quest of everyone I teach to be the best they can be. I don't believe people need a lot of coaching. For me, the game is becoming too mechanical and this is taking the fun out of the game, as people become too tight and too technical. This only serves to create uncertainty and doubt which interferes with their natural swing and ability. Like Palmer, Player, Snead and Norman, I like to keep things simple and help people use their own natural talent to improve their game.

CHAPTER 12

Finding love again

IT WAS ONE OF THOSE MAGICAL THINGS WHICH BEGAN THE first time I saw Isabel Enright coming down the fairway for a lesson. 'She looks pretty good,' I thought. And we just clicked. I don't know why, but it was instant for both of us.

Isabel was from Rosanna Golf Club. She was playing in a guest day at Metro with a friend who had suggested she should have a lesson. She wasn't busy that afternoon, so she came across to the practice fairway and that was the beginning of it. Even though I had given thousands of lessons, both before and after Shirley, I had never felt any chemistry with any one of them until then.

Isabel started having regular lessons with me. She came once a fortnight for three months. Then one day she said: 'Look Brian, I've got two tickets to the theatre. Would you like to come?' We went to the show and had dinner together and that's how it started, and how it kept going. I thought I should be the one to ask her out, and I could have, but it was still very awkward for me as she was a member. I was so glad when Isabel took the initiative. After that she came for a lesson every day.

We went out together for a year before I told the family. I knew it would be difficult. Isabel was a perfectionist and everything had to be 110 per cent right. I knew my children would have trouble with this. They had never been close to 100 per cent right.

I finally introduced them to each other one Saturday afternoon. Isabel and I we were watching the 1979 Victorian Open, which was at Metropolitan, and I brought her in for a cup of coffee when the children were home. I just said: 'This is my new girlfriend,' and it went off very well.

'Dad had a new lease of life with Isabel. The beauty of it was that Mum had hated golf and didn't come from a golfing family, while Isabel did. It was wonderful for Dad to have someone he loved, and who loved golf too, because we kids didn't either.'
Sadie Ann Heizer, daughter

The kids were very surprised about our romance and even a bit shocked that they hadn't been told earlier. They were pleased for me, and even more so that I had found a golfing soulmate.

It was difficult in the first few months and remained difficult. Isabel took the girls out for lunch and for shopping, and then we introduced the kids to Isabel's two sons, Michael and Stephen, then 29 and was 27. We had our first combined Christmas that year. I tried to keep the kids happy and Isabel happy, but unfortunately the two families didn't ever really mix, and we just had to work around it.

Brian and Isabel on their wedding day

'Brian had a wonderful, calming, easy going influence on Mum and she helped him keep track of things. At home, she started refurbishing straight away, and in the business, Mum had been raised in a successful family retail business and knew how to keep the books. I remember her surprise and annoyance when she first saw the pro shop books and saw how many members owed Brian money. Brian was unfazed though, he was never materialistic and was sure it would all work out in the end.'

Stephen Enright, stepson and Metro member

Isabel with Stephen Enright, circa 1985

As we were both Church of England (Anglican), we were married, again by Metro member Canon Russell Clark, at St Andrew's in Bentleigh, where Isabel's sister attended, on 8 January 1981.

We drove to Sydney for our honeymoon and stayed and played golf at Mollymock and in Sydney for five days, because that was all the time I could take off. We were a great team. We both had a lot of energy and were perfectionists in sometimes opposite ways.

Meanwhile, my kids were 20, 18 and 15 by then and ready for the next stage of their lives. I remember Sadie Ann saying: 'Look, Dad, you go your way, we'll go our way and we'll just split the difference.' We did get on very well in the finish, though.

Sadie Ann was the first to leave home. She went to live in a unit with three other girls and later married Robert Heizer, and Susie married Ken Gracey in 1980. Andy went to work at Bond University in Queensland, married Nikki there and has stayed in Queensland ever since. They all turned out to be very wonderful children and have remained very close to each other. Over the years they have given me seven beautiful grandchildren: Susie has Benjamin and Simone, Sadie Ann has Charlie and Georgia, and Andrew has Jesse, Levi and Leah. I have also enjoyed watching Stephen's children, Daniel, Nicky, and Jessica grow up.

Golf tours to UK

My new life with Isabel coincided with new opportunities to travel. In 1980, I was asked to take a group of 30 Metropolitan people to the Open. This started several years of fun trips to the Open, in 1980, 1982, and 1984 when Seve Ballesteros won at St Andrews. We also went in 1986, 1990 and 1994. It was wonderful to have Isabel with me on these trips.

Brian at Sunningdale, 1980

After the first two years, when I ran the trips myself for Metro members, a company called Trident Travel in Pascoe Vale approached me to lead tours for them. It was a great relationship. We would have a conference and I would select the clubs and the itinerary, while the company did all the organising, advertising and bookings. The company attracted the people, but I had to understand and manage them.

The trips were for three weeks. We'd arrive in London, and go straight on to Edinburgh and play 18 holes. After being on the aircraft for more than 24 hours, we wouldn't go to bed. We'd play the 18 holes and then it would be back to normal. That's the trick. Never go to sleep. Just go and play, get tired and let your body get back to normal.

Playing out of the rough at Turnberry, 1984

We played all over Scotland. We played and stayed in magnificent places such as Glen Eagles, Turnberry, Muirfield, Dalmahoy Country Club in Edinburgh, St Andrews and so many other courses. We did two weeks in Scotland and one week in Ireland, where we played Ballybunion, Royal Dublin, Tarlee and Lahinch.

We played 21 games in 25 days. It wasn't too much. When you are on holiday, all you are doing is playing golf, eating and going to sleep. Everyone did their own thing at the end of the tour. Some would go on to travel in Europe while others went straight home.

After the three weeks, I'd have a week off to travel with Isabel and make time to see my family before we came back.

The Twite family from left: Keith, Nigel, Wendy, Brenda, Brian, Sadie, Sylvia (Mum), Daphne, Shirley, Eileen, Theresa and Basil (Terry was absent) in King's Lynn, Norfolk, 1984

I always got some attention from the local newspaper when I came home, which we all enjoyed.

Whenever I could, I would also go back to Sunningdale to visit my greatest teacher and mentor Arthur Lees. I loved introducing Isabel to Arthur and Sunningdale too and we went back more than once.

GOLFER BRIAN BACK FROM OZ

Brian Twite (second left) tees off with his family, including new arrival Benjamin (centre). (90/5836).

THIRTY-FIVE years after emigrating top play golf in Australia, Brian Twite returned to his Leziate home last week.

Mr Twite professional at the prestigious Metropolitan Golf Club in Melbourne, was in England on tour with a group of Australian golfers, culminating in a trip to the British Open Championship.

Before jetting off to Paris and Rome, he managed to fit in a few days with his family, including his 10-day-old great-nephew Benjamin.

Joining 63-year-old Mr Twite on the trip was his wife Isobel.

Mr Twite's golf career began as a caddy at the old Leziate course, and he graduated to assisting Ryder Cup player Arthur Lees at world-famous Sunningdale. This week he visited Mr Lees — now in his eighties but still golfing.

During his spell in Australia, Mr Twite has won many valuable tournaments, including the Victorian State Championship.

Article in the local newspaper, 1990

Golfing friends and Cobram holidays

Once she became a member, which took a long seven years, Isabel made friends at Metro easily and widened my social circle.

We so enjoyed the dinners and trips away with many golfing friends. We first started going away to play golf with Kay and Geoff Leeton, and Bill and Helen Kimber, more than 20 years ago. It was

Kay's idea. She made Isabel a hat for the races one year when they went to Oaks Day, and Kay suddenly thought, 'Why don't we all go away together?' We went to Swan Hill for first two years and then Cobram, which was closer. Then we were joined by others who became regulars, among them Kim and Jenny Hoff and Roger and Belinda Yelland, from Royal Melbourne. Jenny

Brian with Arthur Lees at Sunningdale, 1980

Peardon joined us, as did Lisa Parkinson and Alan Wain, who began by just driving me up there and have now joined the group as regulars. We all get on so well together and, in any one year, we will have sixteen players at Cobram.

Kay has been magnificent. She organises everything, from the tee times to the trophies. We have a four-ball better-ball every day, and nearest-the-pins, and we all bring some prizes for the trophy pool. I always have a grudge match with Roger, too. As soon as he sees me, he says: 'Right, Twite, I'm gonna beat you.' And I say: 'Oh, no you're not.' And he never does, but we both enjoy the rivalry. I love these trips. I have only missed one year, last year, when I was laid up with a knee reconstruction.

Ann and Tony Johnston would always come to visit us at Cobram and have a chat. It's always been wonderful to see them and their three wonderful sons as they grew up. Everyone at Cobram has always been so friendly and welcoming, year after year.

Isabel playing at Flinders Golf Club in May 1991

CHAPTER 13

Retiring from Metropolitan – briefly

WHILE I WAS DEVOTED TO TEACHING AND TO METROPOLITAN and it had been my life for so long, I felt it was time to spend more time with Isabel. Being a professional's wife does have its disadvantages, and although she didn't complain, Isabel did have many 'life after golf' plans in mind. While I was still feeling young at 68, we decided in 1994 that it was time to have more time for each other, for our family and to experience more of the world beyond golf.

The year 1994 was a turning point for changes in other parts of the club, too. The committee replaced the manager, Alan Harwood, with Allan Shortland, previously the house manager, and appointed a young Richard Forsythe as the course superintendent. The committee also wanted to take over the pro shop and run it themselves. When they later appointed the new pro, Ross Anderson, a young highly qualified assistant professional from Kingswood, he worked as a member of staff rather than run the pro shop as an independent business as I had done.

Farewell dinner

The club put on a magnificent retirement dinner for me which was a tremendous success. I was deeply honoured when the captain, Geoffrey Knorr, awarded me with a life membership and a magnificent painting by Bob Wade of the 18th hole. For me, this was the ultimate recognition I could receive for my 39 years of service to the club. It meant I really must have been doing a good job. It also meant that I could play in all the club events, including board events, if I ever wanted to. I was happier to play on Wednesday afternoon, and sometimes on a Saturday. As a golf professional I didn't think, back then, that it would be right to compete with members for the important events in the club. I'm happy to play now because I can't win.

There were further wonderful speeches and much laughter, including a very clever poem and pretend knighthood from Peter Hey, inspired by the A.A. Milne poem, 'Bad Sir Brian Botany'.

GOOD SIR BRIAN TWITEY

Sir Brian was a golf pro and Metro was his home
He went among the members and taught them how to play
On Tuesday and on Saturday, but mostly on the latter-day
He'd call up all his pupils and this is what he'd say
    I am Sir Brian, swing low
    I am Sir Brian, chat chat
    I am Sir Brian, now let your swing flow
    It's this, and this, and that.

A Night To Remember . . .
Brian's Farewell Dinner

Left to right: Brian with Val Maine, former captain Ken Stonier, Betty MacLachlan and Peter Hey, from the Metropolitan Newsletter, 1994.

Captain Geoff Knorr with Brian

– CHAPTER 14 –

Building a new life

To begin our new life, Isabel and I built a house at 13 Lister Avenue, in Sorrento, on the Mornington Peninsula. It was designed by a very expensive architect in Rye and built by Tim Rollings. All the houses in the street were built by Rollings and it was a wonderful house and a lovely place to live. It was right on the top of a hill, half a mile from the beach, so we could see all the ships coming up the Bay.

The golf was wonderful, too. We Joined the National and Flinders, and then Geoff Brash put us up for membership at Sorrento. We were in heaven, but we couldn't keep up with them all, so we let Flinders and the National go, and just played at Sorrento.

My favorite thing about living in Sorrento was that we could go anywhere. We'd go to Flinders for lunch or across to Queenscliff on the ferry. There are just so many wineries, golf courses and friends; we couldn't want for more.

We still came back to Melbourne every week. Isabel played at Metro every Tuesday

'Isabel always played in front of me and when we got to the 13th tee, she would always be sitting there having won her match. So I decided to join her and won many of my matches on the 12th too. I remember one woman at Kingswood saying "'I was hoping to see more of this course." We won three pennants during those years. We must have had a good coach.'

Jenny Brash, past captain and Metro member

From left: Mrs D. Dunn, Mrs D. Johnson, Mrs G. Donnan (Capt), Mrs W. Pitcher, Mrs R. Farrar, Mrs G. Brash, Mrs B. Twite, Miss J. Allen, 1983

and came back to town on Fridays to play pennant with great friends Jenny Brash and Win Johnson.

I came back to teach at Golf Park, on Warrigal Road near South Road, in Moorabbin. I needed to keep teaching and to look after the many golfers from Metropolitan and other clubs who wanted to keep having lessons. I worked there for four days a week for five years.

I didn't retire. I couldn't retire. I had to continue teaching or I would be dying. Even though it was a lot of driving, it suited me. That was until one day when Allan Shorland and club captain Alan Wilkinson asked me if I'd like to come back and teach three days a week at Metropolitan. I accepted immediately. The timing was perfect because Golf Park was about to be demolished to make way for the proposed Dingley Bypass.

I was so happy to be back at Metro because that's where I felt I belonged more than anywhere. With my spare days, I continued to teach one day a week at Trueman's Driving Range in Rye. I played golf at the weekends and managed to teach juniors once a month on a Sunday, and the regular children's clinics three times a year. I am still as busy as I can be teaching. When I am not teaching or playing, I am just resting and preparing for the next day's golf – that's all I want to do.

As we were so often travelling back and forth between Melbourne and Sorrento, Isabel found a beautiful apartment in Hedgley Dene Avenue, in East Malvern, which we both loved. Instead of coming up every Tuesday, we planned to stay there for two days and Sorrento for the remainder of the week.

Trueman's Diving Range at Fingal on the Mornington Peninsula

Losing Isabel

I could see that Isabel wasn't right long before we knew she was really sick. She used to get tired and would be short of breath when we played golf, which wasn't like her. Isabel had always been very energetic and healthy and very interested in living the healthiest life she could. I was very proud of her when, aged 61, she was one of the few in her year to complete a degree course in naturopathy, which was a great achievement.

It was a terrible shock when we took her to a specialist to be told she had lung cancer. He told me privately that people with this type of cancer normally lasted only one or two years. Isabel had never smoked a day in her life, but she had already lost her one brother at 67 and her sister at 69 to cancer. As they grew up, they had worked in their father's hardware shop, the biggest in Footscray, and lived with lead paint and the fumes of chemicals and played in asbestos dust and helped cut sheets of it when they were older. The oncologist said they would have all died from asbestos-related cancers. Isabel was 74. The whole thing was so quick – she was diagnosed in December 2005 and died in June 2006.

'When Isabel first became sick and was struggling in any way, Brian would be there. He had always kept an eye on her. He loved her to bits. One day when we were playing, he went over and helped her out of a bunker. She took a moody turn, fearing that everyone would think she was on the way out, or something like that. She said: "Go away, Brian. I can do this." Of course, two months later, she was in hospital and dying. It was way too fast. For someone who had such a clean life, and never smoked, she gets that rare type of tumour, and has no chance. It was so unfair, so hard on Brian. I've seen a lot of relationships, but those two really had the real love relationship. It was a match made in heaven.'

Kay Leeton, friend and
Metro member

Isabel didn't want anyone to know she was ill, including the family, for as long as possible. So I couldn't tell my children and she only told her sons in her last six months. As I have said before, Isabel was 110 per cent perfection, and this was one thing she wanted to do on her own, in her own way, and we respected that. I did everything I could while I could and, thankfully, she never had any physical pain. I can talk about it now, but at the time I just had to live and work through the grief as best I could. I had done it before and I had to do it again. I kept working, kept my routine, and, with the support of close friends, that's what kept me going. It's no good sitting at home weeping or sulking. You've got to get out there and work to keep busy. You've got to be doing something that you like to keep your mind occupied while the time passes. For me, I kept my mind on teaching and it took me 12 months to get over the hardest grief. I had had 25 wonderful years with Isabel for which I will be forever grateful.

Returning to Melbourne

After the funeral, which was attended by a huge crowd at St John's Church on Point Nepean Road, it was time to leave Sorrento and return to Melbourne. I couldn't live there without Isabel and the house was part of her estate. With the help of my stepsons, Stephen and Michael, we sold the house and renovated the apartment in town exactly according to Isabel's plans.

I remained teaching at Metro and Trueman's range, in Rye, which kept me going. My family and friends also kept me going during those first years, and still do. New friends, like Lisa Parkinson and Alan Wain, came along, too. They started having lessons with me in 2005 at Golf Park. Both their respective parents had played golf and knew of me, and so did Alan, who grew up near where I used to run clinics at

Lakes Entrance. When Lisa was finally ready to start playing golf and found me, everyone was very supportive. Through the regular lessons, first at Golf Park and then at Metro, I suggested they became Metro members, and we became friends outside of golf as well. We continue to play golf and have dinner together at least once a week and have travelled a lot together too.

Travelling again

Lisa and Alan started by driving me to the annual Cobram trip, and to the Leongatha Brian Twite Bowl, and they soon became regulars in the Cobram group. We had such a good time together that we started going further afield. We went to Barnbougle and Port Fairy, Barwon Heads and across to New Zealand. The really big trip was to the UK and Europe in 2012. We went to Sunningdale, of course, and I wanted to visit King's Lynn where I could introduce Lisa and Alan to the family. I also wanted them to play some of my favourite courses – Birkdale, Troon, Turnbury, Prestwick, Dornoch and St Andrews.

I was very pleased to be able to visit my sister, Maureen Brosious, in the United States as part of the 2012 trip. As the visit was a late idea, and I hadn't been to the States for 26 years, I didn't know I needed a

Port Fairy, 2010

Cape Kidnappers, New Zealand, 2009

14th at the Old Course Sunningdale, April 2012

18th at Royal Birkdale, where Brian shot his age, 85, 2012

Brian with Alan Wain in front of the clubhouse at Chantilly, France, April 2012

visa until I got there. It looked like I was going to make it past the Philadelphia airport staff until a big fellow came across, and asked: 'What's the problem here?' One of the staff said; 'This guy hasn't got a visa. He can't come in.' 'Give me your passport', the big man said.

He looked at my passport and landing papers and then said; 'Oh, you're a golf professional.' I nodded. 'How long have you been teaching?' I said: 'Oh, about 60 years.' He asked me to follow him and when we were out of earshot, he said: 'I've got a slice. What shall I do?'

I dutifully showed him how to fix his problem and he got me my visa.

Somehow some people from the media found out I was in the country and came to interview me at my sister's place. Instead of being rejected and sent back to the UK, I was photographed and interviewed as a 'legendary golf professional' and my story was written up in a local newspaper.

This was my last trip and, as such, my last chance to say farewell to the people and places that have meant the most to me in the United Kingdom and America. I am so grateful to have had this opportunity and to have had this opportunity and to have been able to do it with such good friends in Lisa and Alan.

'Brian is such an easy traveling companion and he would often surprise us. Wherever we went, he would attract attention. In every pro shop, especially here and in New Zealand, someone would know him, or know of him, and the conversations would flow. He was a golfing celebrity and, as he had a natural rapport with everyone, we always had a good time socially. We also learnt quickly that Brian is not a tourist; he was there only for the golf. If we suggested a visit to a famous castle on the way to a golf course, he would say in his resolute way: "I'll wait in the car." Even in Paris, he could not be distracted for long. On the first day, we did a double-decker sight-seeing bus tour and were making plans for day two when he announced that we had "seen" Paris and we should get back to golf. We duly made an unscheduled trip with golf clubs via the Paris metro and a taxi to the nearest golf course, Chantilly Vineuil.'

Lisa Parkinson, friend and Metro member

CHAPTER 15

Being honoured

I HAVE SPENT MY LIFE TEACHING AND IT'S BEEN MY MISSION. I love helping people improve and receiving reports that they've lowered their handicap by four shots or they have achieved a certain goal that was important to them. I love hearing about their successes and their increasing enjoyment of the game.

For me, the best reward you can have in teaching is feedback and recognition. Positive feedback confirms that my teaching fundamentals are correct, my method of teaching is correct and that the player has done what has been asked of them and practiced it. The system has worked on both sides and that gives me a lift. A lot of people who have lessons never practice even if you keep at them all the time. They don't improve so you don't get any thrill from them.

Teaching has therefore given me the best rewards I could ever want. It has kept me going for the past 70 years and still does. I couldn't have a better job – to do what I love doing every day and be paid for it. Being capable of helping thousands of people play golf is also the thing I'm most proud of and where I get my inner joy of teaching from.

As a teaching professional of such longevity, I have also been rewarded with public recognition far beyond anything I could possibly imagine. Sometimes, it has come from the most unexpected sources.

Rubbing Shoulders with the Greats – Golf Tips and Tales, 2010

I used to teach Evan Spargo, a long-time Metropolitan member, who became a great friend. He was an excellent golfer, played off scratch and was in the pennant team. One day, he and fellow member and professional Cameron Strachan asked me: 'Hey Twitie, why don't you write a book about the way you teach?' They interviewed me a dozen times, recorded it and that's what we came up with. Evan and his wife, Carmen Ferrari, did a very good job and I hope everyone enjoyed reading it.

The book was published and launched at the club in November 2010. We still have copies for sale in the pro shop at Metropolitan and new members are given a copy when they join the Club.

The PGA awards

I was delighted when the Victorian PGA (Professional Golfers' Association) recognised my great friend Jack Harris and me by naming The Jack Harris & Brian Twite Victorian PGA Seniors Foursomes Championship after us. Given we were both quite senior at the time, this was very fitting.

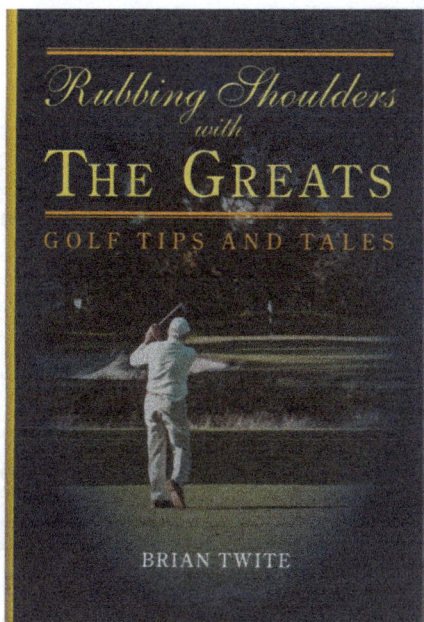

*Dressed up for the Presentation Dinner with great friends Bob Wade
and Alasdair MacGillivray, 27 November, 2010*

I was further delighted to be recognised in the PGA Australian
Centenary Awards in 2011. I was in very good company, being one
of the 28 PGA professionals from across Victoria recognised for
their contribution to Australian golf and the PGA across a number
of areas, including playing and coaching. The list of Victorian
recipients included: Robert Allenby, Stuart Appleby, Steve Bann,
Michael Clayton, John Davis, Ian Denny, Bruce Devlin, Trevor
Flakemore, Stewart Ginn, David Graham, Bruce Green, Jack Harris,
Michael Harwood, Graham Kelly, Peter Knight, Harold Knights, Kel
Llewellyn, Dale Lynch, Howard McHutchison, Paul Moloney, Tim
Moore, Geoff Ogilvy, Bob Shearer, Brian Simpson, Ian Stanley, Peter
Thomson, Brian Twite and Russell Wilson.

The Victorian Golf Industry Hall of Fame 2013

I was also in excellent company when I was inducted into the Hall
of Fame on 4 June 2013. The list that year included three-time
Australian Open champion Ossie Pickworth, David Graham, Susie
Tolhurst (Metro), Harry Williams, Gladys Hay (Metro), The Hon
Michael Scott, Eveline McKenzie, Joan Fisher (Metro), Mick Ryan,
Nellie Gatehouse, Margaret Masters (whom I had taught briefly) and
Kevin Hartley.

It was a great night. Over 20 people from Metropolitan attended
the Hall of Fame dinner and presentations. My lifelong friends such
as the Kimbers, Leetons, Knorrs, Raddens and many more, and also
quite a few young fellows, were there to support me.

Order of Australia 2013

The ultimate recognition I could ever have as a citizen of Australia was
to receive the Medal of the Order of Australia. I knew three months
beforehand but couldn't even tell my daughters. It's a secret and you
can't tell anybody until it's in the newspapers on the day.

Finally, on 28 January 2013, I received my OAM for 'service to
the sport of golf as an administrator and mentor'.

Of course, I don't use the title, but it was an honour beyond any
expectation and quite something for a little kid from Leziate who had
thought the gift of a new set of golf clubs was beyond belief. I donated
the medal to the Club, and this is where it belongs. It was my long
association with Metropolitan that has allowed me to achieve all I
have in teaching and promoting junior golf, and it will stop any rows
in the family over who keeps it when I am gone!

Brian Twite OAM receiving the award from the Governor of Victoria,
The Hon. Alex Chernov AC QC at Government House, 2013

The Trainee Professionals' Tournament

Closer to home, I was thrilled when the Trainee Professionals' tournament, held at Metro every year, was named after me in 2016. This is now one of my favourite days. They know how much I love supporting our trainee staff in the pro shop, and the funds raised go support our junior program at Metro – perfect.

Hitting off the first in the 2017 Brian Twite Trainee Professionals' tournament

Being 90

I was deeply honoured again when the club hosted a 90th birthday party for me on 19 August 2016. We had a wonderful night in the new clubhouse, with moving and funny speeches. Weston Bate even wrote a poem for me and it's not the first time the poets in the club have been moved to celebrate in verse. There was so much 'Metropolitan love in the room', as they say, that night.

Indeed, I couldn't love my club more or be more proud of its members, who really are the most gracious hosts. Metropolitan has always had a fine reputation for the course and for its members since I arrived in 1955, every guest that comes to Metro for a game receives the same warm welcome and respect as if they were members. They not only think the course is magnificent, they love the atmosphere too. And as for the members, I am sure we are all having a longer and happier life for being here. It's just magnificent!

Completing my days at Metro

A few years ago, to be closer to Metropolitan, I sold the apartment and moved to a new unit in Cameron Avenue, South Oakleigh. It's just two minutes from the practice fairway where I continue to teach a few days a week. More than that, it's built on original Metropolitan land as I knew it when I first arrived in 1955 before the subdivision.

This is where I belong, and this move symbolises and completes my life circle at Metropolitan. Over my 63 years here, I have lived in the clubhouse, on the old and the new 17th, and now I look forward to seeing out my days on the old 16th.

Looking ahead, I just want to stay fit, so I can play three or four times a week and still teach. I feel great and think I can keep going like this indefinitely – it's been a great formula so far!

After I'm gone, my children might think I should be buried with Isabel down at Sorrento, but I think I should be cremated, with my ashes scattered on the practice fairway to annoy everybody else. Perhaps save some to scatter under the big flowering gum next to the clubhouse.

I have spent most of my life at Metropolitan, so that's where I should finish.

Brian Twite

I've written a poem, but realise that my title, simply *Brian Twite*, may be insufficient for this royal and ancient golfer. To add a string of names to match his regal status, I have given him Brian, Bright, Polite, Forthright, Delight and the hyphenated family name, Hitswith-Skilanstrength Twite.

As firm and forthright as he stroked the ball,
He made the pro-shop central to a sense
Of what it meant to be at Metropolitan,
And earned respect from everyone
Who came into his care. His observations
Of untidy swings brought apt adjustments,
Building confidence. No drastic steps!
His voice was calm! Even the best
Found nourishment from tips
Dropped in their path. And strugglers
Made improbable improvements.
And, more than that,
He showed us all, with Shirley and Isobel,
That life's greatest game
Could offer better than birdies
Every day.

Brian writes of rubbing shoulders
With the greats. But from that contact
Much rubbed off on them.
About the value of a golfing life.
He was as great as those he hosted here;
Ben Crenshaw, with his fluent putting stroke;
Resourceful Player or imposing Norman;
His mentor, Arthur Lees, colourful Trevino,
And so precise Von Nida.
He saw it all and understood
What made them tick. And they were glad
To know him and receive droplets of wisdom,
As, of course, have all of us.
Those droplets, over many years,
Became a wave on which the spirit of golf has surfed.
We've been completely blessed by knowing him.

Across the world, in leading golfer's minds
A single name will conjure Metropolitan.
And that is Brian Twite,
Of great delight.

Weston Bate
19 August, 2016

Ideally, I'd like to die on the course after sinking a 20-foot putt on the 18th green to win the match. Then I'd be finished.

And after I'm gone, I just want to be remembered as a guy who did his job as well as he possibly could, and the only thing I want people to say about me is that I was a good fellow. That will be enough for me.

THE END

My life lessons

Like my approach to golf, my approach to the fundamentals of life has always been straightforward and uncomplicated. My parents, golf teachers and my life have taught me everything I have needed to know to live a happy and fulfilling life. When I have been asked, I say the most important lessons I have learned, from the beginning, include the following.

Tell the truth. My mother taught all twelve children never to tell an untruth. If you told an untruth, it cost you knuckles with a cane. She used to say, 'Children, if you go through life telling the truth, you can't go very far wrong.' To me, that's been in my life all the time. However, there is still a place for telling the 'truth' people need to hear to allow them to believe something that's very important to them. For example, like the time I made a set of clubs for Doc Priestly. He hated them, and said, 'They were the worst set of woods I've ever had!'. All I did was change the colour to allow him to believe they were different, and he loved them. I never had the courage to tell him.

Never speak badly about a person or speak in anger. If you criticise or say something bad about somebody it always finds a way back to that person which is never a good thing. My mother also used to say when you were cross with someone, 'Count to ten before you speak'. I learnt this very early and found it was very successful when I was resolving disputes between my sisters. By the time they had counted to ten, one slowly and the other quickly, the tension was released, and we could solve the issue.

Be honest with yourself – don't think you are better than you are. Don't get an ego. I never let myself think I was above anyone else. Again, this comes from my mother's upbringing. If you thought you were better than somebody else, she'd knock that out of you in two minutes. She'd hit you across the knuckles and say, 'You're not! You're no different than that person.' I was also trained from my young caddying days to Sunningdale to know my place in the scheme of things.

Look after yourself. I learnt this being one of twelve children. You had to work out what you wanted and how to get it and to be confident in who you are. That's why I joined the navy. I thought it would be exciting and it was. The Navy also taught me to look after myself, to be self-reliant and ready for anything.

Be yourself, believe in yourself. Everybody has to be themselves, accept who they are, and believe in themselves to be the best golfer and person they can be. They must find and play with their own unique swing and strengths, stay true to that, and not try to copy others or be something they are not.

Respect yourself. Don't let the old guys get on top of you. I also learnt early on as a young club professional not to let other people disrespect you. Arthur Lees used to say, 'Hey Brian, if anybody complains, get in there first. Don't let them get in. You get in there first,' and it worked. One day I was having a practice round at Victoria when Mr Merrick, the manager, came out and shouted, 'I'll see you in the clubhouse, Twite, when you're finished.' He was mad because we were playing off the back tees, and we shouldn't have been. I walked up to his office, and knocked, was invited in and there he was sitting behind the desk with a glass of whisky.

I said, 'Hello, Mr Merrick. I've never been spoken to on the golf course or anywhere like you've spoken to me today. I was in the navy for four years and even the officers didn't speak to me like that. Now what's the bloody problem?' 'All right, sit down', he said politely. We were great friends after that. If he was at Metro, he always came to the shop to talk to me. He was an excellent manager. He controlled the golf course. He controlled everything. He was good.

Do the right thing. A keenness to do the right thing has always motivated me – not much you can add to that.

Concentrate on the present. The biggest lesson you learn in life is that you must concentrate on the present and not on the past. You must forget the past. You've got to think of the present. If you don't do that, you're no good. General Robinson first taught me that at Victoria when I couldn't concentrate after we ran over Googie Withers' dog. I had to learn it again when I lost Shirley and Isabel.

Purpose of life. For me, my purpose in being alive is to become a better person, and the purpose of my life's work has always been to help other people to be the best that they can be too, on and off the golf course. I know I have been a good father to my kids, and if I had to choose a symbol to sum up my role in life, it would be to be a father to everybody, without the collar of course.

No regrets. I have always been happy to accept where I am and have loved what I have been doing and where I have been doing it. I have never wished for a different life or a different path. How could I wish for more – if you're happy with yourself and you're happy with what you're doing, and for me it was working at a golf course like Metropolitan which is at the top of the class, where else do you want to go? There's nothing else to do. I taught all sorts of people and they all came back, some whom I gave lessons to over 40 years ago. They only come back for a talk, not so much a lesson.

Mary Thomson, Peter's wife, asked me over dinner one night if I would change anything. With a straight face, I said, 'There is only one thing Mary, Peter's

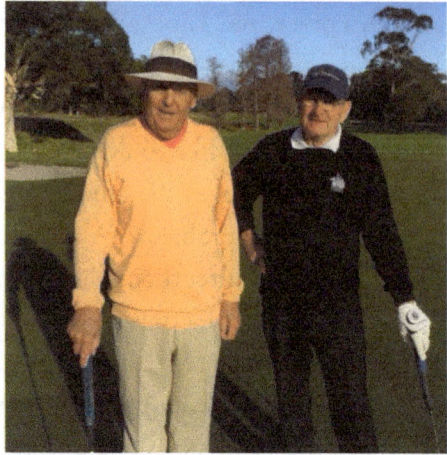

Brian with Terry Twite on 17th at Metropolitan, June 2018

birthday is on the 23rd of August, same as me, but he's three years younger. If only he had been born three years earlier, and I had been born three years later, I would have been the British Open Champion and he could be the best teacher.' She said, 'Well, Brian, that doesn't happen.' What I've done in my life in the Navy and in teaching, I couldn't think of anything better. I have no regrets whatsoever.

Brian with Sadie Ann and Susie, South Oakleigh, 2017

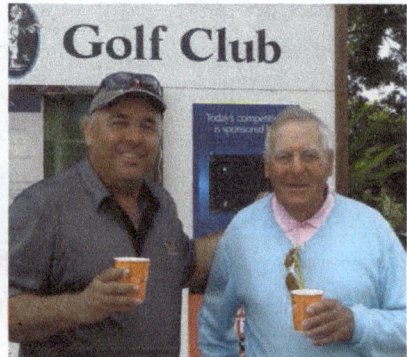

Brian with Andrew Twite at Tweed Heads Golf Club, 2014

Technical fundamentals and fixes

The swing fundamentals

The full swing

I have based my swing fundamentals on what I learnt from my first teacher Jack Lovelock at Leziate, which have been confirmed over the years and I have added to as new ways of saying the same thing were needed.

1. Grip – if you haven't got a good grip, you can't play golf. It's that simple, both 'V's (the 'V's are the lines between thumb and first finger when gripping the club) must point up to the right shoulder.

2. Head – keep your head and eyes still.

3. Swing – thumbs up to the sky at waist-high, take your arms around you, and know where the clubhead is throughout your swing.
4. At impact – your head must look over your right shoulder when you hit the ball, so you stay behind the ball. Don't allow your head to get ahead of your shoulder. On the back swing, have your head, left shoulder and left knee in line and when you hit the ball, have your head, right shoulder and right knee in line.
5. Follow through – when completing your swing, always think or mentally say, 'and finish' as Gary Player always said.
6. Confidence – be confident in what you are doing and stay true to these fundamentals. If you start fiddling with your swing and are not confident, everything falls apart.

Chipping

Chipping is simply a shorter swing to hit the ball a shorter distance; the fundamentals are much the same as for longer shots. The distance is controlled by the loft on the club, the length of the swing and the speed of the clubhead or how hard or fast you hit the ball. You can also adjust each club by closing the club face and pressing the hands forward to play a lower shot with more run, or you can open the face to create a higher shot and make is stop quicker. A short chip to the hole can also be played as a long putt but with a more lofted club. Unlike a putt, however, you must remember to pick the club up on the backswing not keep it low to the ground or you will hit thin or fat shots – the clubhead must always come back square to the ball.

The important thing when you're chipping is that both hands must be together. There's no wrist movement, no twisting or turning. The right hand is always behind the left. Like Jason Day, who is

Brian Twite instructing a member at Metropolitan, 1955

magnificent. When you watch Jason Day, his right hand is always behind his left – the right hand never passes the left.

Ideally, players should spend at least an hour a week on chipping which can be the hardest part of the game for most club golfers. The easiest chip, and the safest one, can be done with the lowest loft so the ball runs closest to the ground like you are rolling a lawn bowl. The higher lofted wedge shot should be used only when needed, when a bunker must be carried for example, or you need to stop the ball quickly. For this shot, play the ball at the back of your stance and hit the ball firmly with a firm grip and both hands working together to create backspin. For really lofted shots, you can play them more like a bunker shot by opening the face and using a bunker swing.

Bunkers

To get the greatest loft on your greenside bunker shots, keep your left shoulder lower than your right so you don't get too much sand, open your stance and the face of your club, and have the ball and your hands forward. On the backswing break your wrists up quickly and take the club up high. On the downswing, hit the sand about two inches behind the ball, you keep your lower part as quiet as you can, so your shoulders and arms are together, and follow through with your arms with a slow, soft swing. The swing shape looks like a big 'V'. Vary the distance behind the ball and the speed of your swing to vary the length, and to allow for soft and heavier sand. As a rule, I think *club, sand, ball*, to hit the sand first and to visualise splashing the ball out of the sand.

On long bunker shots, you look at the front of the ball because you want to hit the ball first and grip the club about one and a half inches down the shaft. I also recommend that your keep your head high, so you don't hit too deeply into the sand. I think *club, ball, sand* in fairway bunkers to help hit the ball first. Using a hybrid or a lofted fairway wood can also be a good option on a long bunker shot if the lie is firm.

Adapting the fundamentals to the lie

Bad lies

If it's a bad lie, either an uneven or a loose lie, you need to hit the ball with the toe of the club, not with the heel. If you hit it with the heel, the whole club hits the ground at the same time, but if you hit it with the toe of the club you've only got a half inch of the toe of the club that's going to hit the ground. There's less resistance, so the clubhead just goes through. You just turn the toe in. Instead of having the blade square you turn the toe in by closing the face.

Divots

Rather than try to hit down on the ball to get out of a divot, which can often lead to fat shots, hover the club half an inch above the ball at address and keep it there through the swing, and you will still hit the middle of the ball.

Sloping lies

The main key to all sloping lies is to keep your balance. To keep your balance, you put your knees forward and stick your bottom out and sit there and swing with your arms. Bad shots are all caused by the legs moving too quickly on the downswing. They must stay absolutely still. Balance is the key to every side slope, upslope, bunker shot, low shots, high shots, in fact everything.

Down slopes

Swing the club so it follows the slope downhill and maintain your height through the swing. To do this, set up and adjust your stance to lean forward so your shoulders are parallel with the slope, keep your weight on the right side to stop you moving forward, and watch the front of the ball so you hit the ball first. If the slope is steep, you can also play a more lofted club, because the slope may tend to close the face turning your 8 iron into a 7 iron for example.

Up slopes

Set up with the ball in line with your left heel, your shoulders parallel to the ground and your weight on your left side so you can't fall backward and watch the back of the ball. Then swing the club up the slope, not into the slope. Again, you may choose to play a stronger club to counter the upslope.

Side slopes

If the lie slopes away to the right, aim a little to the left to keep it straight and vice versa. For a side- downslope, play the ball off your back foot, bend your knees, stick your bottom out like your sitting on a chair, put your shoulders down and keep your shoulders at the same level all the way through the swing so you don't come up when you hit the ball. You may also need to have your hands a little higher to allow for the downhill slope.

If the ball is above your feet on a side slope, drop your hands and cock your wrists according to how high the slope is, so it may look more like a baseball swing. If you use a normal swing, you're going to hit six inches behind the ball. Alternatively, you can shorten the shaft by gripping the club lower on the grip.

Plugged ball in a bunker

Close the face of your sand iron, play if off your back foot, hit down on the back of the ball and stop. The ball will pop on to the green – no follow through is necessary.

Ball under water

Similar to other bad lies, turn the toe of your sand iron in 1 inch so only the sharp end of the club, the toe, will have to get through the water to hit the ball. Play the ball off your back foot, pick up the club sharply to shoulder high, and swing down firmly with your left hand leading to hit very hard on the back of the ball and follow through.

Adapting the fundamentals to the situation

Low shots

To hit a low ball under trees or branches, use a low lofted club, hit the top two thirds of the ball and keep the blade square.

High shots

To hit a high ball over trees or branches use a higher lofted club and hit the bottom of the ball. This will open the face adding 10 degrees to the loft and helping it sail high into the air. Similarly, hitting down on the bottom of the ball helps lift shots out of fairway bunkers with a high lip.

Fades and draws

To hit around trees and draw the ball flight from right to left, simply hit on the outside of the ball, or a 5 o'clock as this will close the face on impact and will give you a 10- to 15-foot draw. To fade the ball from left to right, hit the ball on the inside at 7 o'clock as this will open the face and give you a 10- to 15-foot fade without changing anything else in your swing.

Punch shots

Punch shots are great into the wind, or when for any reason you can't complete a full swing. Grip the club half an inch down the shaft, put the ball at the back of your stance, have your right shoulder higher than your left, and keep all your weight on the left side. Keep your shoulders still and play this shot with your arms only. Again, you must not let your legs move ahead of the ball.

Swing fixes – returning to the fundamentals

Swaying

Moving or swaying during the swing is one of the most common problems and causes the most grief on the golf course. Sadly, swayers keep forgetting this. For example, I've got a girl from Sorrento who rings me up every two or three months to say, 'Brian, I'm cutting the ball again.' I say, 'Oh, yes. I know your swing,' and my mind goes back to all the lessons I've given the girl. She goes from a twenty-four handicap, gets down to sixteen, then she goes to twenty-four because she moves a mile. I say, 'For God's sake do what I tell you. Put your left side next to a kitchen bench and swing your arms through without hitting the kitchen bench with your arms or your body.' 'Oh, yes. I've forgotten that,' she agrees. She just needs to pivot around her spine instead of swaying or transferring her weight from front to back and into the bench.

It's the same when you're throwing a ball – you never throw your weight forward; seventy per cent of your weight remains on your right side. Arthur Lees did this sixty years ago. He had the whole Ryder Cup team throwing balls thirty, forty metres for a half an hour before they hit a ball because when you throw a ball you're not thinking, 'Turn the shoulder, turn the hip, do this and do that.' You just throw the ball naturally, and then when you put a golf club in your hand you do the same thing. Swinging a club is very simple if you allow yourself to swing the club with your natural ability.

Throwing from the top

Releasing the club too early or throwing from the top is another costly problem. If you release too early, the hit is weak at impact, which is also called a power-leak. It means that the right hand has passed over the left on the downswing. This is caused when the right arm gets too close to the body and your left hand collapses. The same applies when the right elbow breaks too early, causing the left arm to break also and that's when you hit from the top.

To counteract this, keep both arms straight on the backswing until you get past your right knee and then you can break your right elbow. Most bad shots in swinging are caused because the right elbow breaks too early on the backswing. Both hands should be strong at the top, and never let the right hand dominate at the top.

Slicing the ball

Slicing is caused by moving the arms and body ahead of the clubhead, or by swinging outside in, which means the club is open at impact. This can happen when we are trying too hard to hit the ball, when the player is tired, especially at end of the round, and when hitting into the wind or under pressure. The opposite is the answer – less effort, and a shorter, slower swing are better under pressure from the weather or from the score.

Technically, a slice is created when the left arm is too strong, and it pulls the club across the ball before the club head can catch up. By slowing down the arms, everything falls into balance and the ball can be hit square in the middle and go straight.

A slice can also be caused by throwing from the top. If your left arm is bent at the top of the swing, this allows your right elbow to bend too quickly and then when the right arm straightens at the top of the swing and throws the club outside the line. Alternatively, if you're hitting from the top, you can slice it or even hook it with the same swing depending on how fast your hands are at the ball – slower hands will open, and faster hands will close the club at impact.

All bad slices are caused when the club hits through the ball from 5 o'clock to 11 o'clock, (outside in) instead of 7 o'clock to 1 o'clock (inside out), where 6 o'clock is the centre back of the ball. You must keep your arms away from your body on the downswing and hit from inside out. Most people think about bringing their hands down to the ball to hit it. But it's not the hands, it's the club head that has to hit the ball.

Hooking

Hooking the ball is another major problem for club golfers and affects more men than women. Instead of keeping the right shoulder and right arm behind on the downswing, the right shoulder and arm come over the top. This makes an outside in swing plane, the ball is hit with a closed face which creates a hook, or a straight pull to the left if the hands are fast enough. The remedy is to keep the club head behind your hands on the downswing and think again of how you throw a ball or skip a stone across water – your hand is always behind the ball or stone when you throw it.

Topping the ball

Topping is caused when there is too much body movement and your weight moves forward off your right side too early and your shoulders. Missing the ball altogether, the air shot, happens when you are too tight in the shoulders, and you lift your head. To hit the ball correctly, you must be balanced through the swing and be as balanced on your finish as when you started.

The dreaded shank

Shanking occurs when you are too close the ball and the club is taken too far inside the line on the backswing. Your swing then becomes too cramped and you have no room to swing your arms through freely. You make space by moving your body out of the way too early ahead of the club head which then comes through too open at impact. The ball is hit with an open leading edge and flies off to the right which can be so alarming. There are many cures, but all require different swing thoughts and practice. You can practice by standing just on your right leg, so your arms can get through freely, or you can hit with only one hand, so the two hands aren't fighting each other – most people hold their left hand too tightly. You can practice keeping the left hand soft and flexible enough to release, or let the right hand dominate on impact and the follow-through. Some people have to work through all the strategies to reclaim their balance and their confidence to put all thoughts of shanking out of their minds.

Stuck in the bunkers

If you can't get the ball out of a bunker, try setting up with your left shoulder lower than your right shoulder, and watch the back of the ball. You can also turn your head slightly to the right, so you look down at the back of the ball with your left eye, and then make sure you hit the ball and swing through past your chin. Although its best to take your backswing straight back or even outside the line, make sure you hit the ball from inside out. If you hit it with the heel, because your right hand has come over the ball, the ball will run along the ground or be shanked. Swing inside out and hit down on the ball to make it rise, and let the right hand dominate through impact and the follow through to the hole. Make sure your shoulders and arms move together and keep your lower body quiet. It's the easiest shot after you do all that!

My most successful swing fixes

Hitting a line-up of balls

The most successful thing I do to hit the ball correctly is to put a dozen balls in a row and just walk along the line and hit them. This is the simplest thing I do to teach people to hit the golf ball. It works so well with children who aren't having any fun trying to hit the ball but missing it. There was a five-year-old crying, and I said, 'What's up?' 'Oh, she doesn't like it,' said the parent. I said, 'Look. Let's make this exciting.' So, I put six balls in a row, walked along the line and I went, bang, bang, bang, bang, bang, bang. 'Oh!' she said, 'This is fun.'

One group of Korean kids I was asked to teach at Golf Park weren't allowed to do a full swing until they had hit thousands of balls on the practice fairway from waist high to waist high for three months. After that they really knew how to hit a golf ball. They could swing the club anyway they liked but would always know how to get the club head back to the ball. Many youngsters get fixated on making the swing work, but the swing is only a part of the system.

Getting your rhythm back

If your rhythm is upset for any reason, it could be a bad shot or two, a missed putt or a lost hole, it's vital that you recover your balance and your confidence as soon as possible. Seventy per cent of all problems can be technically fixed with one simple solution – the right hand and right knee must work together on the downswing. When the club gets down to waist high, the right hand and right knee must move together as one unit. It's the same when you throw a ball, the right arm and right knee come through together to release the ball. This will get you back on line. If the right hand is too quick you will top it, and if it's too slow you will slice it – they must come through together.

The putting fundamentals and strategies

Putting was the weakest part of my game when I was young, and I didn't have the sense to practice and make putting a priority. I spent hours and hours just driving thousands and thousands of balls on the tee with the driver. So, for my long game, I would be off say 2 + and for my short game, chipping and putting, I would be off about 6. I didn't concentrate much on my putting because I didn't have to – I could hit every green in regulation or less and I could hit any club close to the hole. However, as you get older and your shots get worse, your putting does get better, and so has mine.

While putting is the shortest shot in golf, it is the most used club and has the biggest impact on your score, and the fundamentals are basically the same as the full swing. However, because putting has more to do with confidence and feel than the longer game, there is far more room for individual preferences and idiosyncrasies. As people seek to become better putters or fight the dreaded putting yips, technical aids and fads come and go from time to time. For example, taking the club straight back and straight through square to the ball without following the natural arc or hinge of the swing. This was popular in the 1970s and again recently until players find that it doesn't work for them.

From my experience over the years, I teach several key putting fundamentals and some advanced strategies for keener putters, all of which have stood the test of time.

1. Grip – you can use any grip you like but good putters tend to have a light or soft grip.

2. Stance – for maximum balance, your feet should be slightly open and shoulder width apart. Your head should be over the ball which should be about 12 inches out from you and 12 inches inside your left foot. Again, good putters can stand however they like and still be good putters.

3. Keep still by keeping your eyes still – this is the most important thing to do as moving is one of the biggest causes of missed putts. Where you put your eyes can vary, you just have to be consistent. You can focus on the front of the ball, in front of the ball or in front of the hole or focus on the back of the ball exactly where you want to hit it with your putter blade.

4. Where to hit the ball – this is key and there are three main options here. You can hit the ball at either 5 o'clock, 6 o'clock (centre back) and 7 o'clock. Arthur Lees and Gary Player taught me this method. For a right to left putt, you open the blade slightly, half

an inch, and hit the ball at seven o'clock so you're cutting the ball against the borrow. When it gets to the hole, it doesn't run away with the borrow because it's slowing up and fighting the curve. For a left to right putt you get the opposite effect by closing the face slightly and hitting the ball at 5 o'clock. With a straight putt, of course, you hit the ball in the centre at 6 o'clock. You can use these options to allow for the grain too.

The girls do this a lot more than the fellows at Metropolitan or the youngsters who think it's old hat. They think you should take it straight back and straight through with a square blade but when you get them on the putting green and especially on the right-hand side of the green where it's downhill and you get them to putt and they hit it and they go 10 feet past the hole and then I hit mine and it goes a foot from the hole, 'Oh yes, but I hit mine too hard,' they say – they've always got an excuse. It's not just the amateurs; Lee Trevino wouldn't change his putting method for the extra fast greens on the final day and it cost him a tournament here – he three putted four of the last nine holes. Karrie Webb doesn't like Metro greens because when she comes home and plays in Queensland the greens there are slow and thick, she can bump them. She left herself with so many four-foot putts when she played here because she was trying to hit it into the hole, instead of coaxing it in, and it didn't work. It takes confidence and practice to be able to trust this method when it really counts, and some people don't want to bother but it really is the best way of handling fast and undulating greens.

The best and most consistent putters, Nicklaus, Player and Palmer, never varied their putting. They might have had a bad day, but they never had a bad year because they concentrated on hitting the ball in relation to where they wanted to go on the green. In other words, they knew how to get the ball in the hole. They only looked at the part of the ball they wanted to hit. As Palmer said to me, 'Just think of the part of the ball you want to hit. Don't worry about what your hands or arms are doing. Just make the club hit the part of the ball you're thinking of.' It's just so simple. It's the same when you use a hammer. You don't think about how you're going to swing a hammer. You only think what part of the target you are going to hit and how hard you want to hit it.

5. How to hit the ball – the best putters are tappers. This means hitting the ball and having a short follow through so the putter head parts with the ball as soon its hit. Many short putts are missed when the putter stays too long with the ball on the follow through. To practice this, I used to hit the ball and immediately bring my putter back to make sure I had parted with it.

6. Lining up – hit to the line you first see, not to the hole. As Jack Lovelock told me when I was 10, 'When you go on the green, son, you look at the line, hit the ball on the line that you first see. Never walk around the hole and imagine that there's borrow on the line. Your first impression is the one.' I never do anything else. I've never gone around and looked at 15 angles. As soon as I walk on the green I look at the hole and I look at the ball, two inches left, for example, that's my line, that's my hit.

    If you can't see a line, read it as straight and nine times out of ten it's correct. If you do see a line, you hit it on the first line you see. I look at the ball and I look at the hole and my first impression tells me how far I'm going to hit it left or right. I pick a line, I hit it along the line, and use my putter blade to help minimise the borrow.

7. Gauging the distance – first thing you do on the putting green is assess how long the putt is. Is it 5 feet, 2 feet, 10 feet, or 20 feet? Once that's in your brain and you can visualise the putt, your brain tells you how hard to hit the damn thing. You don't just look at it and say, 'Oh this is a long putt' and hit it or you will have loose ends on how hard you want to hit it. If you feel you can't measure the distance on the green, think of something that you see every day, such as a car length or the length of your kitchen bench, or use something you have with you such as the length of your putter shaft.

8. Managing very fast putts – if you have a fast-downhill putt, hit the ball with the heel of the club, and hit it normally. It doesn't matter what shape your putter head is, using the heel will minimise the speed of the ball and will take 4 feet off a 20-foot putt. Alternatively, you can open the face slightly to slow the ball down, and you can do the opposite for uphill or very slow greens. You can also slow the ball down by putting your hands behind the ball. Most people put them forward and this is why people hit the ball superfast sometimes, which they should do on slower greens. If you put your hands behind the ball, the club gets to the ball before your hands get to the ball, and this is also the simplest way of stopping the yips.

Fixing the yips

The yips – jerking the club off line when putting – is the most dreaded of all putting problems and can take the longest to fix as a player's confidence can be completely lost. Technically, it is most often caused when the left arm and hand are so tight that the right hand can't hit though the ball, so the putts miss on the right, or the right hand is too dominant which pulls your putts to the left. There are a few ways to correct these imbalances.

1. Bend the left arm and keep the arm soft to allow the right arm to go through the ball.

2. Keep the heel of the putter in front of the toe of your putter blade – this will stop the right hand turning over the left. The right hand should never pass over the left whether it's driving, chipping or putting. I do this by having my putter blade slightly open. This ensures that my right hand starts behind or is under my left at address and stays behind when I hit the putt. Kel Nagel, the most wonderful putter, was the same. He always had his putter slightly open. The secret in putting in short putts, or in any putt, but in short putts mostly, is never to allow the toe to past the heel as you hit the ball.

3. Keep your hands behind the ball to allow the club to get to the ball before your hands. This is similar to keeping your right hand under your left – it stops the right hand jerking over and across the ball.

4. Always focus on the part of the ball you want to hit and hit it. Don't focus on what your hands and arms are doing. When you miss putts, don't overthink or start doubting your ability, or your stroke, or you will just make things worse as you mind starts to fight with your muscles and your natural swing. Just focus on the part of the ball you have selected and hit the ball to your target, and you will soon see a drop in the number of putts you have per round.

These are the things that have worked for me and my pupils. With putting, however, it's such an individual thing, players ultimately have to find their own best methods.

CONTRIBUTORS

Sincere thanks to the individuals and organisations listed below for their time, stories and other invaluable contributions to this book.

Players

Paul Ansell	Dr Kay Leeton	Gary Player
Michael Bannenberg	Pam Kelton	Corrie Perkin
Debbie Baulch	Dr Bill Kimber	Steve Perkin
Jay Bethell	Helen Kimber	Dr Bryan Radden
Kit Boag	Dick Kirby	Alan Reiter
Clyde Boyer	Trevor Lockett	Colin Reiter
Jenny Brash	Peter Lothian	Graeme Reiter
Michael Clayton	Alasdair MacGillivray	John Ross
Sue Clark	Val Maine	John Smith
Jeffrey Collinson	Fance Morrell	Helen Stead
Chris Faram	Caroline Nicholson	Robert Wade OAM
Bruce Fordham	Patricia Owen	Alan Wain
Marcus Harty	Lisa Parkinson	Sandie Wright

Family Members

Stephen Enright	Sadie Ann Heizer	Terry Twite
Susie Gracey	Andrew Twite	Wendy Twite

Golf club historians

John Churchill, Sunningdale Golf Club
Chris Reeks, King's Lynn Golf Club
Jon Smith, Leongatha Golf Club

CONTRIBUTORS

Golf organisations

The Metropolitan Golf Club
Peter Paccagnan, General Manager
Anthony O'Brien, Hospitality Manager
Adam Smith, Golf Operations
Moira Drew, Archivist

Golf Victoria
Karen Harding, magazine editor

The Golf Society of Australia
Graeme Ryan, President

The PGA
Gavin Kirkman, CEO

Printed in May 2019
by Rotomail Italia S.p.A., Vignate (MI) - Italy